THE INCREDIBLE NEW YORK YANKEES TRIVIA BOOK

THE INCREDIBLE NEW YORK YANKEES TRIVIA BOOK

300 QUESTIONS FOR THE SUPER-FAN

DAVID FISCHER

Sports Publishing books may be purchased in bulk at special discounts for sales promotion, corporate gifts, fund-raising, or educational purposes. Special editions can also be created to specifications. For details, contact the Special Sales Department, Sports Publishing, 307 Fifth Avenue, 4th Floor, New York, NY 10016 or sportspubbooks@skyhorsepublishing.com.

Sports Publishing® is a registered trademark of Skyhorse Publishing, Inc.®, a Delaware corporation.

Visit our website at www.sportspubbooks.com.

10 9 8 7 6 5 4 3 2 1

Library of Congress Cataloging-in-Publication Data is available on file.

Cover design by David Ter-Avaneysan
Cover photos credit: Getty Images

Print ISBN: 978-1-68358-531-2
Ebook ISBN: 978-1-68358-532-9

Printed in the United States of America

Contents

Introduction vii

Chapter 1: From Pinstripe Origins to the House That Ruth Built 1

Chapter 2: The Iron Horse and the Yankee Clipper 15

Chapter 3: Mantle's Era and a Decade of Dominance 29

Chapter 4: The Bronx Zoo 43

Chapter 5: The Core Four 55

Chapter 6: Legendary Moments 69

Chapter 7: Notable Rivalries 81

Chapter 8: The Modern Era 93

Chapter 9: Leaders of the Pack 105

Chapter 10: Fun Facts 117

Introduction

Welcome to *The Incredible New York Yankees Trivia Book*!

At the start, I admit to not being a fan of the word *trivia*, as it alludes to unimportant facts or information of little use. Nothing can be further from the truth. As someone once said, "What I know is knowledge. What I don't know is trivia." In other words, even the most erudite Yankees fans can be stumped by a question so esoteric, so obscure, so arcane, so trivial that it defeats the purpose of engaging in discussion. Because the best trivia questions might be the ones with no one answer. I much enjoy sitting around with friends when one asks, "Name the Yankees Opening Day lineup in 1996." Correctly answering seven of nine makes you a real fan; even if you didn't get all nine, there's no shame in that. A real baseball fan knows more than just the answer to a question. Who hit the Shot Heard 'Round the World? That's Bobby Thomson, of course. But a true fan knows the pitcher was Ralph Branca, who replaced Don Newcombe. That Willie Mays was the on-deck batter. That the two baserunners were Clint Hartung and Whitey Lockman, because Hartung was pinch-running for Don Mueller, who hurt his ankle sliding into third base.

To repeat, none of this information is trivia. It's knowledge. And don't I know it.

I hope you enjoy testing your knowledge of the New York Yankees as much as I enjoyed creating the test. It's my hope that the questions and answers will unlock wonderful memories of the players and games that make baseball the best sport in the world.

Good luck and have fun!

FROM PINSTRIPE ORIGINS TO THE HOUSE THAT RUTH BUILT

QUESTIONS

The Roaring Twenties marked the dawn of a golden age for the New York Yankees, transforming the franchise into a legendary dynasty and establishing a winning culture that would last into the next century. The era was defined by the team's move to the iconic "House That Ruth Built," Yankee Stadium, in 1923. That same year, they won their first World Series title. This period was anchored by the incomparable talents of Babe Ruth, acquired in 1920, whose prodigious home runs captivated the nation and changed baseball forever. The 1927 squad, arguably the greatest team in history, dominated the sport, marching to a World Series championship with unmatched power and skill, cementing the Yankees' status as baseball's premier team. Throughout this chapter, your knowledge of the team's earliest days will be tested. But always, keep your cool. Should you answer a question incorrectly, please don't curse the Bambino.

1. What was the franchise's nickname from 1903 to 1912 before becoming the Yankees?
A. Gothams
B. Highlanders
C. Knickerbockers
D. Metropolitans
Answer on page 11.

2. Which was the first home field for the American League's New York franchise from 1903 to 1912?
A. Astor Place
B. Hilltop Park
C. Madison Yards
D. Metropolitan Stadium
Answer on page 11.

3. Who led the American League in wins with 41 in 1904, setting the franchise record for most wins in a season?
A. Jack Chesbro
B. Clark Griffith
C. Al Orth
D. Jack Powell
Answer on page 11.

4. What minor league team did Babe Ruth play for before joining the Boston Red Sox?
A. Akron Bulldogs
B. Baltimore Orioles
C. Durham Bulls
D. Toledo Mud Hens
Answer on page 11.

5. Which Yankees pitcher surrendered Babe Ruth's first career home run while Ruth was still a member of the Boston Red Sox on May 6, 1915?
A. Ray Caldwell
B. Jack Chesbro
C. Ray Fisher
D. Jack Warhop
Answer on page 11.

6. Name the colonel who along with Tillinghast L'Hommedieu Huston purchased the Yankees for $1.25 million on January 29, 1915.
Answer on page 12.

7. Name the distinctive uniform design that first appeared on the Yankees uniforms in 1912.
Answer on page 12.

8. Who was the first Yankees pitcher to throw a no-hitter?
A. Ray Caldwell
B. George Mogridge
C. Bob Shawkey
D. Urban Shocker
Answer on page 12.

9. Where did the Yankees play home games prior to the construction of the original Yankee Stadium in 1923?
Answer on page 12.

10. Who was the Boston Red Sox owner who traded Babe Ruth to the Yankees after the 1919 season?
A. Harry Frazee
B. Walter O'Malley
C. Bill Veeck
D. Tom Yawkey
Answer on page 12.

11. Which was the future Pro Football Hall of Famer allegedly displaced in the outfield by Babe Ruth when Ruth joined the Yankees for the 1920 season?
A. Red Grange
B. George Halas
C. Bronko Nagurski
D. Jim Thorpe
Answer on page 12.

12. In what year did the Yankees win their first American League pennant?
Answer on page 12.

13. Which player hit the first home run at the original Yankee Stadium in 1923?
A. Lou Gehrig
B. Tony Lazzeri
C. Babe Ruth
D. Whitey Witt
Answer on page 12.

14. Which journalist was the *New York Evening Telegram* sportswriter who dubbed Yankee Stadium, "The House That Ruth Built?"
A. Heywood Broun
B. Fred Lieb
C. Damon Runyon
D. Grantland Rice
Answer on page 12.

15. In what county of New York State will you find Yankee Stadium?
Answer on page 12.

16. Name the manager who guided the Yankees to their first six American League pennants and three World Series championships.
Answer on page 12.

17. Which pitcher surrendered Babe Ruth's record-setting 60th home run on September 30, 1927?
A. Bump Hadley
B. Walter Johnson
C. Firpo Marberry
D. Tom Zachary
Answer on page 13.

18. Which pitcher was the only 20-game winner for the 1927 Yankees?
A. Wilcy Moore
B. Herb Pennock
C. Urban Shocker
D. Waite Hoyt
Answer on page 13.

19. Which batter led the 1927 Yankees in hits?
A. Babe Ruth
B. Lou Gehrig
C. Earle Combs
D. Bob Meusel
Answer on page 13.

20. Four members of the 1927 Yankees knocked in 100 runs, including Lou Gehrig, Babe Ruth, and Tony Lazzeri. Who was the fourth player?
A. Earle Combs
B. Joe Dugan
C. Mark Koenig
D. Bob Meusel
Answer on page 13.

21. Which pitcher won 18 games for the 1927 Yankees while dealing with heart issues that would take his life the following year?
A. Waite Hoyt
B. Wilcy Moore
C. Herb Pennock
D. Urban Shocker
Answer on page 13.

22. Name the National League team the Yankees beat to win the 1927 World Series.
Answer on page 13.

23. To date, the 1927 World Series is the only World Series to end in this fashion. How did the winning run score?

A. Balk

B. Catcher's interference

C. Sacrifice fly

D. Wild pitch

Answer on page 13.

24. Two pitchers from the 1927 Yankees are in the Hall of Fame. One is Waite Hoyt. Which pitcher is the other?

A. Wilcy Moore

B. Herb Pennock

C. George Pipgrass

D. Bob Shawkey

Answer on page 13.

25. Name the second baseman of the 1927 Yankees who was inducted into the Baseball Hall of Fame in 1991.

Answer on page 13.

26. What nickname was given to the 1927 Yankees because of the team's incredibly powerful and feared lineup?

Answer on page 13.

27. Why did Babe Ruth wear uniform jersey number 3?

Answer on page 14.

28. Which Chicago Cubs pitcher surrendered Babe Ruth's famous "called shot" home run in Game Three of the 1932 World Series?

A. Burleigh Grimes
B. Bobo Newsom
C. Charlie Root
D. Lon Warneke

Answer on page 14.

29. Which Detroit Tigers pitcher surrendered Babe Ruth's 700th career home run?

A. Elden Auker
B. Tommy Bridges
C. Firpo Marberry
D. Schoolboy Rowe

Answer on page 14.

30. For which team did Babe Ruth hit his 714th and last home run?

A. Boston Braves
B. Boston Red Sox
C. New York Yankees
D. Pittsburgh Pirates

Answer on page 14.

31. Which actor portrayed Babe Ruth in the 1992 feature film *The Babe*?

A. Chris Farley
B. James Gandolfini
C. John Goodman
D. John C. Reilly

Answer on page 14.

32. Name the outfielder who hit for the cycle three times during his Yankees career from 1920 to 1929.
Answer on page 14.

FROM PINSTRIPE ORIGINS TO THE HOUSE THAT RUTH BUILT

ANSWERS

1. B—Highlanders. The American League's Baltimore Orioles franchise, which played from 1901 to 1902, folded and was replaced by the New York Highlanders in 1903.

2. B—Hilltop Park. The home ballpark was dubbed Hilltop Park because it was located on one of the highest spots in the borough of Manhattan.

3. A—Jack Chesbro. In addition to 41 wins, Chesbro also led the league in games started (51), complete games (48), and innings pitched (454 2/3) in 1904.

4. B—Baltimore Orioles. In 1914, Ruth was signed by the minor league Baltimore Orioles, but was soon sold to the Red Sox.

5. D—Jack Warhop. In only his 18th major league at-bat, Ruth hit a solo home run by slamming a third-inning pitch from Warhop into the right-field stands at the Polo Grounds. Ruth collected two more hits that day and pitched 12 1/3 innings before taking the 4–3 loss to the Yankees.

6. Jacob Ruppert. Ruppert owned the Yankees until his death in 1939.

7. Pinstripes. Pinstripes created a look that would become the most famous uniform design in sports.

8. B—George Mogridge. Mogridge threw a no-hitter in a 2–1 win at Fenway Park on April 24, 1917.

9. Polo Grounds. The Yankees played in the Polo Grounds, home of the National League's New York Giants, from 1913 to 1922.

10. A—Harry Frazee. Frazee's sale of Ruth starts "The Curse of the Bambino."

11. B—George Halas. Halas appeared in only 12 games for the Yankees in 1919 before embarking on a legendary pro football career.

12. It was 1921. The Yankees were defeated by the New York Giants in the 1921 World Series five games to three. The Series was a best-of-nine that season.

13. C—Babe Ruth. On Opening Day in 1923, Ruth went yard for the first homer hit at the old Yankee Stadium. He went on to smash 41 that season.

14. B—Fried Lieb. Lieb's 70-year career culminated with his being honored by the Hall of Fame in 1973 with their career excellence award.

15. The Bronx. Yankee Stadium is located at One East 161st Street in the Bronx, the northernmost of New York City's five boroughs.

16. Miller Huggins. Huggins managed the Yankees for 12 seasons, from 1918 to 1929.

17. D—Tom Zachary. With the game tied in the eighth inning, Ruth connected off Zachary for a two-run homer in the Yankees 4–2 win over the Washington Nationals.

18. D—Waite Hoyt. Hoyt posted a 22–7 record in 1927.

19. C—Earle Combs. A leadoff batter and center fielder, Combs recorded a team-leading 231 hits in 1927.

20. D—Bob Meusel. Gehrig had 173 RBIs, Ruth 165 RBIs, Lazzeri 102 RBIs, and Meusel had 103 RBIs in 1927.

21. D—Urban Shocker. Posting a record of 18–6 with a 2.84 ERA in 1927, the thirty-seven-year-old Shocker died from pneumonia and heart disease on September 9, 1928.

22. Pittsburgh Pirates. The Yankees outscored the Pirates 23–10 and won in four straight games in the first sweep of a National League team by an American League team.

23. D—Wild pitch. The Yankees won the Game Four clincher in the bottom of the ninth inning when Johnny Miljus's wild pitch sent Earle Combs home with the Series-ending run.

24. B—Herb Pennock. Pennock finished with a 241–162 record during his 22-year career. He was a part of four World Series-winning teams with the Yankees and was a perfect 5–0 with a 1.95 ERA in 10 World Series games.

25. Tony Lazzeri. Lazzeri played for six Yankees pennant winners from 1926 to 1937, batting .293 with ten seasons of 80 or more RBIs during his 12 years in pinstripes.

26. Murderers' Row. The fearsome nickname described a lineup so deep and incredibly powerful that pitchers struggled to get through it.

27. He batted third in the lineup. Back then, players were assigned numbers based on their position in the batting order.

28. C—Charlie Root. In the fifth inning, Ruth made a pointing gesture with his hand before clubbing Root's pitch deep over Wrigley Field's center field wall.

29. B—Tommy Bridges. Ruth connected in the second inning of a 4–2 Yankees win at Detroit's Navin Field on July 14, 1934.

30. A—Boston Braves. Playing for the Braves, Ruth's final home run came in a game in which he hit three homers against the Pittsburgh Pirates at Forbes Field on May 25, 1935.

31. C—John Goodman. Other actors to portray Ruth include William Bendix in the 1948 film *The Babe, Ruth Story*, Max Gail in the 1984 TV movie *The Babe*, and Stephen Lang in the 1991 TV movie *Babe Ruth*. Bob Meusel.

32. Meusel hit for the cycle—a single, double, triple, and home run in the same game—at Washington on May 7, 1921, at Philadelphia on July 3, 1922, and at Detroit on July 26, 1928.

THE IRON HORSE AND THE YANKEE CLIPPER

QUESTIONS

The New York Yankees of the 1930s and 1940s extended the dynasty built in the 1920s, achieving remarkable success despite the Great Depression and World War II. The era saw a transition of power, from the legendary Babe Ruth to a new generation of stars. The team's offense was consistently potent, featuring the likes of the formidable Lou Gehrig and the emerging phenom Joe DiMaggio, who debuted in 1936. The Yankees won five American League pennants and an unprecedented four consecutive World Series titles from 1936 to 1939—a feat unmatched by even the great teams of the Ruth era. The decade concluded with the poignant retirement of the "Iron Horse," Lou Gehrig, in 1939 after his ALS diagnosis, a poignant moment etched in baseball history. This chapter contains several very difficult questions. Should you answer them all correctly, you can consider yourself to be one of the luckiest people on earth.

33. Which college did Lou Gehrig attend?

A. Columbia University
B. Fordham University
C. Hunter College
D. New York University

Answer on page 25.

34. Name the Yankees first baseman who lost his job to Lou Gehrig after he took himself out of the lineup because of an alleged headache on June 2, 1925.
Answer on page 25.

35. Lou Gehrig's streak of 2,130 consecutive games played began on June 1, 1925, when he pinch-hit for which teammate?
A. Earl "The Kentucky Colonel" Combs
B. "Jumping" Joe Dugan
C. "Silent" Bob Meusel
D. Paul "Pee-Wee" Wanninger
Answer on page 25.

36. Who replaced Lou Gehrig as the Yankees' first baseman on May 2, 1939, ending his 2,130 consecutive games played streak?
Answer on page 25.

37. Select the screen actor whose stoic portrayal forever immortalized Lou Gehrig in the 1942 film, *The Pride of the Yankees.*
A. Gary Cooper
B. Clark Gable
C. Cary Grant
D. Jimmy Stewart
Answer on page 25.

38. Lou Gehrig's streak of 2,130 consecutive games played stood as Major League Baseball's record for 56 years, until September 6, 1995. Who eclipsed Gehrig's streak?
Answer on page 25.

39. True or False. Lou Gehrig is the Yankees' all-time franchise leader in triples.
Answer on page 26.

40. Hack Wilson of the Chicago Cubs set the Major League Baseball single-season record for most runs batted in, with 191 in 1930. The next year Lou Gehrig set the American League single season RBI record. How many RBIs did Gehrig have in 1931?
A. 158
B. 166
C. 173
D. 185
Answer on page 26.

41. Who was the first Yankees manager to be honored with a monument?
A. Frank Chance
B. Bill Donovan
C. Clark Griffith
D. Miller Huggins
Answer on page 26.

42. Name the Pacific Coast League team from which the Yankees purchased Joe DiMaggio for $50,000 on November 21, 1934.
Answer on page 26.

43. Name the Yankees infielder who, on May 24, 1936, became the first player in Major League Baseball history to hit two grand slams in one game.
Answer on page 26.

44. Whose .362 batting average in 1936 was the highest batting average recorded by an American League catcher for over seventy years?
A. Bill Dickey
B. Joe Glenn
C. Aaron Robinson
D. Buddy Rosar
Answer on page 26.

45. Who won the pitchers' Triple Crown in 1937 for the second time in four years?
A. Spud Chandler
B. Lefty Gomez
C. Red Ruffing
D. Monte Pearson
Answer on page 26.

46. Who led the American League with 27 stolen bases in 1938?
A. Frankie Crosetti
B. Babe Dahlgren
C. Leo Durocher
D. Red Rolfe
Answer on page 26.

47. The Yankees lineup in Game Four of the 1938 World Series featured five future Hall of Famers, including Joe DiMaggio, Lou Gehrig, Bill Dickey, and Red Ruffing. Name the fifth player who would become a Hall of Famer.
A. Frankie Crosetti
B. Joe Gordon
C. Tommy Henrich
D. Red Rolfe
Answer on page 26.

48. Name the manager who guided the Yankees to seven World Series titles, including four in a row from 1936 to 1939.
Answer on page 26.

49. Who set a Major League Baseball record in 1939 by scoring at least one run in 18 consecutive games?
A. Bill Dickey
B. Joe Gordon
C. Red Rolfe
D. George Selkirk
Answer on page 26.

50. Who led the American League with 19 saves in 1939, at the time the second-highest total in Major League Baseball history?
A. Spud Chandler
B. Atley Donald
C. Johnny Murphy
D. Monte Pearson
Answer on page 27.

51. Who was the first Major League Baseball player to play on four World Series championship teams in his first four years in the big leagues, the 1936–39 Yankees?
A. Bill Dickey
B. Joe DiMaggio
C. Tommy Henrich
D. Joe Gordon
Answer on page 27.

52. Which song inspired by Joe DiMaggio's hitting streak and recorded by the Les Brown Orchestra climbed as high as sixteenth on the Billboard charts in 1941?
A. "Center Field"
B. "Glory Days"
C. "Joltin' Joe DiMaggio"
D. "The Yankee Clipper"
Answer on page 27.

53. Which Cleveland pitcher along with Al Smith ended Joe DiMaggio's historic 56-game hitting streak in 1941?
A. Jim Bagby Jr.
B. Bob Feller
C. Mel Harder
D. Al Milnar
Answer on page 27.

54. Name the Cleveland third baseman who helped end Joe DiMaggio's record 56-game hitting streak by making two sparkling defensive plays to rob DiMaggio of potential hits.
Answer on page 27.

55. Joe DiMaggio and his brother played together as All-Star Game teammates for the American League squad in 1949. Name Joe's outfield brother.
Answer on page 27.

56. Which Hollywood movie star made international headlines by marrying Joe DiMaggio?
A. Ava Gardner
B. Betty Grable
C. Rita Hayworth
D. Marilyn Monroe
Answer on page 27.

57. Who was the first Yankees pitcher to win the American League Most Valuable Player Award, in 1943?
A. Spud Chandler
B. Atley Donald
C. Joe Page
D. Red Ruffing
Answer on page 27.

58. Phil Rizzuto was a shortstop and seven-time World Series champion with the Yankees during the 1940s and '50s. What was Rizzuto's nickname?
Answer on page 27.

59. Who hit the first pinch-hit home run in World Series history in Game Three of the 1947 World Series?
A. Yogi Berra
B. Tommy Henrich
C. Aaron Robinson
D. Snuffy Stirnweiss
Answer on page 27.

60. Whose spectacular catch for the Brooklyn Dodgers in Game Six of the 1947 World Series elicited a rare display of emotion from the famously stoic Joe DiMaggio?

A. Carl Furillo
B. Al Gionfriddo
C. Eddie Miksis
D. Dixie Walker

Answer on page 27.

61. Which Simon & Garfunkel song features the lyric, "Where have you gone, Joe DiMaggio?"

A. "America"
B. "Bridge Over Troubled Water"
C. "Mrs. Robinson"
D. "The Sound of Silence"

Answer on page 28.

62. Which Yankees batter hit the first walk-off home run in World Series history to win Game One of the 1949 World Series?

A. Tommy Henrich
B. Johnny Lindell
C. Cliff Mapes
D. Gene Woodling

Answer on page 28.

63. Which retired uniform number honors two Yankees catchers?

A. 1
B. 5
C. 8
D. 10

Answer on page 28.

64. How many seasons did Joe DiMaggio and Mickey Mantle spend together as teammates?
Answer on page 28.

THE IRON HORSE AND THE YANKEE CLIPPER

ANSWERS

33. A—Columbia University. Gehrig attended Columbia from 1921 to 1923, playing both football and baseball. He signed with the Yankees on April 29, 1923.

34. Wally Pipp. Pipp was the Yankees' first baseman from 1915 to 1925 and was a two-time home run champion during his tenure. He was sold to the Cincinnati Reds in 1926 and finished his career there.

35. D—Pee-Wee Wanninger. Gehrig flew out to left field against pitcher Walter Johnson in a 5–3 loss to the Washington Nationals.

36. Babe Dahlgren. Dahlgren doubled and homered in the Yankees' 22–2 win at Detroit that day, the first game in 15 years without Gehrig on the field.

37. A—Gary Cooper. The actress Teresa Wright portrayed Lou's devoted wife, Eleanor.

38. Cal Ripken Jr. Ripken's 2,632-game streak began on May 30, 1982. He famously broke Gehrig's record on September 6, 1995, and then extended the new record over 500 more games before voluntarily ending it before a game, coincidentally against the Yankees, on September 20, 1998.

39. True. Gehrig collected 163 career triples. Earle Combs is second with 154.

40. D—185. In addition to 185 RBIs in 1931, Gehrig also led the league with 46 homers, 211 hits, and 163 runs scored.

41. D—Miller Huggins. A monument honoring the late Yankees manager was dedicated on May 30, 1932.

42. San Francisco Seals. DiMaggio had a hitting streak with the Seals that lasted 61 games when he was eighteen years old, in 1933.

43. Tony Lazzeri. Lazzeri's two grand slams came during the Yankees' rout of the Athletics, 25–2, at Philadelphia's Shibe Park on May 24, 1936.

44. A—Bill Dickey. Minnesota's Joe Mauer topped Dickey's mark with a .365 average in 2009.

45. B—Lefty Gomez. Gomez leads the American League in wins (21), ERA (2.33), and strikeouts (194) in 1937.

46. A—Frank Crosetti. Crosetti was a member of seven World Series–winning teams during his 17-year career with the Yankees, from 1932 to 1948.

47. Joe Gordon. Gordon was an MVP, a nine-time All-Star, and five-time World Series winner in seven seasons with New York and four with Cleveland.

48. Joe McCarthy. McCarthy managed the Yankees from 1931 to 1946. He recorded a 100-win season six times.

49. C—Red Rolfe. Rolfe scored at least one run in 18 straight games from August 9 to 25, 1939. Cleveland's Kenny Lofton equaled the record in 2000.

50. C—Johnny Murphy. Murphy led the American League in saves four times, in 1938 and 1939 and in 1941 and 1942.

51. B—Joe DiMaggio. DiMaggio was a member of nine World Series–winning teams in all.

52. C—"Joltin' Joe DiMaggio." Singer Betty Bonney provided the vocals.

53. A—Jim Bagby Jr. DiMaggio finished the game 0-for-3 with a walk against Smith and Bagby.

54. Ken Keltner. Keltner was a seven-time All-Star with Cleveland from 1937 to 1949.

55. Dom DiMaggio. Boston's Dom started the 1949 All-Star Game in right field, Joe started in center field.

56. D—Marilyn Monroe. DiMaggio and Monroe were married on January 14, 1954. The marriage lasted only nine months before they divorced, though they remained close friends until her death in 1962.

57. A—Spud Chandler. Chandler was 20–4 with a 1.64 ERA in 1943. The Cy Young Award honoring pitchers wasn't awarded until 1956.

58. The Scooter. Rizzuto was given that nickname by minor league teammate Billy Hitchcock because he was small and quick, especially his movements around the infield and on the basepaths.

59. A—Yogi Berra. Berra pinch-hit for Sherm Lollar in the seventh inning of Game Three of the 1947 World Series and homered off Brooklyn's Ralph Branca.

60. B—Al Gionfriddo. In the sixth inning, trailing 8–5, the Yankees put two men on with two out when DiMaggio launched a deep drive to left field that a lunging Gionfriddo caught before crashing into the fence near the 415-foot sign. DiMaggio uncharacteristically kicked dirt near second base when he saw the ball had been caught.

61. C—"Mrs. Robinson." Although Paul Simon's favorite player was Mickey Mantle, he didn't use his idol's name. "Wrong amount of syllables," Simon said.

62. A—Tommy Henrich. Henrich led off the bottom of the ninth inning of Game One of the 1949 World Series and hit a game-winning home run off Brooklyn's Don Newcombe to give the Yankees a 1–0 win.

63. C—8. The Yankees retired number 8 for Hall of Fame catchers Bill Dickey and Yogi Berra on July 22, 1972.

64. One season, 1951. DiMaggio and Mantle helped the Yankees defeat the New York Giants in the 1951 World Series. Mantle suffered a career-altering knee injury in Game Two while chasing a fly ball hit by Willie Mays, as he swerved to avoid colliding with DiMaggio, his cleat caught on an exposed drain cover in Yankee Stadium's outfield, causing Mantle's right knee to buckle.

MANTLE'S ERA AND A DECADE OF DOMINANCE

QUESTIONS

The New York Yankees were baseball's defining dynasty of the 1950s, winning six World Series titles and appearing in eight during the decade. Led by charismatic manager Casey Stengel, the team seamlessly transitioned from the Joe DiMaggio era to a new generation of icons, including Mickey Mantle and Yogi Berra. Mantle emerged as a superstar, winning MVP Awards and swatting prodigious home runs, while Berra was a perennial All-Star and three-time MVP behind the plate. The decade was capped by Don Larsen's iconic perfect game in the 1956 World Series, a feat that epitomized the team's dominance as a national powerhouse and constant fixture in the American consciousness. As Casey said, you can look it up.

65. Who recorded two game-winning hits during the Yankees' four-game sweep over the Philadelphia Phillies in the 1950 World Series?
A. Bobby Brown
B. Jerry Coleman
C. Phil Rizzuto
D. Gene Woodling
Answer on page 39.

66. Which Yankees pitcher was on the mound for the final out and recorded the save in both clinching games of their 1951 and 1952 World Series championships?
A. Bob Kuzava
B. Joe Page
C. Allie Reynolds
D. Johnny Sain
Answer on page 39.

67. Name the only Yankees pitcher to throw two no-hitters, both of which occurred during the 1951 season.
Answer on page 39.

68. Mickey Mantle hit his first major league home run against the Chicago White Sox on May 1, 1951. Which pitcher gave it up?
A. Randy Gumpert
B. Billy Pierce
C. Virgil Trucks
D. Early Wynn
Answer on page 39.

69. What was Mickey Mantle's jersey uniform number when he broke into the big leagues as a rookie in 1951?
A. 6
B. 7
C. 11
D. 22
Answer on page 39.

70. Which Yankees player won the 1951 American League Rookie of the Year Award?
A. Bobby Brown
B. Bob Cerv
C. Mickey Mantle
D. Gil McDougald
Answer on page 39.

71. What was Yogi Berra's given name?
A. Carmen Short Berra
B. Lawrence Peter Berra
C. Timothy Dale Berra
D. Xavier Anthony Berra
Answer on page 39.

72. Which starting pitcher, known as the Springfield Rifle, recorded three 20-win seasons and posted a 92–40 record during the Yankees' five-year World Series run from 1949 to 1953?
A. Tom Gorman
B. Tom Morgan
C. Vic Raschi
D. Johnny Sain
Answer on page 40.

73. Where did Mickey Mantle hit a 565-foot home run, considered to be the first tape-measure home run on April 17, 1953?
A. Comiskey Park
B. Griffith Stadium
C. Shibe Park
D. Sportsman's Park
Answer on page 40.

74. Which Yankee drove in the World Series–winning run with a walk-off single in Game Six of the 1953 Series against the Brooklyn Dodgers?

A. Billy Martin
B. Johnny Mize
C. Irv Noren
D. Gene Woodling

Answer on page 40.

75. In 1954, the Yankees acquired pitcher Don Larsen from the Baltimore Orioles in what remains the largest trade in Major League Baseball history. How many players were involved in the deal?

A. 7
B. 9
C. 11
D. 17

Answer on page 40.

76. Which player in 1954 became the first Yankees pitcher to win the American League Rookie of the Year Award?

A. Bob Grim
B. Johnny Kucks
C. Johnny Sain
D. Tom Sturdivant

Answer on page 40.

77. Which pitcher teamed with Allie Reynolds and Vic Raschi to form The Big Three of starting pitchers for the Yankees' five straight World Series titles from 1949 to 1953?
A. Whitey Ford
B. Eddie Lopat
C. Jim McDonald
D. Johnny Sain
Answer on page 40.

78. Name the player who made his major league debut in left field for the New York Yankees on April 14, 1955, becoming the first African American player in the team's history.
Answer on page 40.

79. Which Yankees outfielder recorded a hit in 17 straight World Series games from 1956 to 1958, the longest hitting streak in World Series history?
A. Hank Bauer
B. Joe DiMaggio
C. Mickey Mantle
D. Gene Woodling
Answer on page 40.

80. Which nickname was given to pitcher Edward Charles (Whitey) Ford?
A. Chairman of the Board
B. King of the Hill
C. Leader of the Pack
D. Master on the Mound
Answer on page 41.

81. Which Yankees player set a World Series record by knocking in 12 runs in seven games during the 1960 World Series?
A. Clete Boyer
B. Roger Maris
C. Gil McDougald
D. Bobby Richardson
Answer on page 41.

82. During his 12 seasons as Yankees manager from 1949 to 1960, Casey Stengel won seven World Series championships. Name the only other manager with seven World Series titles.
Answer on page 41.

83. Name the Yankees outfielder who won consecutive American League Most Valuable Player Awards in 1960 and 1961.
Answer on page 41.

84. Which pitcher surrendered Roger Maris' 61st home run of the 1961 season, breaking Babe Ruth's thirty-four-year-old record?
A. Steve Barber
B. Jim Bunning
C. Camilo Pascual
D. Tracy Stallard
Answer on page 41.

85. Name the Yankees pitcher who won the 1961 Cy Young Award and the 1961 World Series Most Valuable Player Award.
Answer on page 41.

86. Which Hollywood legend directed the 2001 film *61** that chronicles the historic home run chase between Mickey Mantle and Roger Maris in the summer of 1961?
A. George Clooney
B. Bradley Cooper
C. Billy Crystal
D. Tom Hanks
Answer on page 41.

87. Who was manager of the Yankees when the team won the 1961 and 1962 World Series championships?
Answer on page 41.

88. Which pitcher surrendered a game-winning home run to Mickey Mantle in the bottom of the ninth inning to decide Game Three of the 1964 World Series?
A. Roger Craig
B. Ray Sadecki
C. Curt Simmons
D. Barney Schultz
Answer on page 41.

89. Mickey Mantle hit a World Series record 18 home runs in his career. Name the batter who is in second place with 15 World Series home runs.
Answer on page 41.

90. Name the Yankees play-by-play announcer during this era whose much-spoken line was "How about that!"
Answer on page 42.

91. Which Hall of Fame pitcher's first career complete game was a no-hitter against the Yankees on September 20, 1958?
A. Bob Feller
B. Bob Lemon
C. Hoyt Wilhelm
D. Early Wynn
Answer on page 42.

92. Which Yankees player won his only American League Most Valuable Player Award in 1963?
A. Yogi Berra
B. Elston Howard
C. Mickey Mantle
D. Roger Maris
Answer on page 42.

93. Which was the nickname given to Mickey Mantle?
A. The Colossus of Clout
B. The Commerce Comet
C. The Goliath of Grand Slams
D. The Maharajah of Mash
Answer on page 42.

94. Which pitcher finished first in the voting for the 1968 American League Rookie of the Year Award?
A. Stan Bahnsen
B. Al Downing
C. Fritz Peterson
D. Mel Stottlemyre
Answer on page 42.

95. Name the former Yankees pitcher who authored the controversial 1970 baseball memoir *Ball Four*.
Answer on page 42.

96. Name the player who the Yankees honored by retiring his jersey number 16.
Answer on page 42.

MANTLE'S ERA AND A DECADE OF DOMINANCE

ANSWERS

65. B—Jerry Coleman. Coleman was a member of four World Series–winning teams with the Yankees (1949–51, 1956).

66. A—Bob Kuzava. Kuzava was a three-time World Series champion with the Yankees. Those were his only two World Series saves.

67. Allie Reynolds. "The Chief" no-hit Cleveland on July 12 and Boston on September 28, 1951.

68. A—Randy Gumpert. Mantle's first career home run was hit in the sixth inning and flew over 400 feet into the center field bullpen at Chicago's Comiskey Park. The Yankees won, 8–3.

69. A—6. Mantle switched to number 7 in August 1951 and famously wore that number for the rest of his career.

70. D—Gil McDougald. McDougald hit .306 with 14 homers and 63 runs batted in during the 1951 season. He beat out Minnie Miñoso of the Chicago White Sox in a close vote. McDougald received 13 votes to Miñoso's 11.

71. B—Lawrence Peter Berra. Berra acquired the nickname Yogi during his teenage years after attending a movie that included a scene in India and a friend thought he resembled the actor playing a yogi, or person who practices yoga.

72. C—Vic Raschi. Raschi, born in West Springfield, Massachusetts, went 120–50 in eight seasons with the Yankees from 1946 to 1953.

73. B—Griffith Stadium. Mantle was batting right-handed when he connected against Washington Senators left-handed pitcher Chuck Stobbs.

74. A—Billy Martin. Martin won the 1953 World Series Most Valuable Player Award as he hit .500 with 12 hits, including the Series clincher. A second baseman, Martin won five championships during his seven seasons with the Yankees.

75. D—17. The Yankees sent a total of 10 players to Baltimore in exchange for seven players, including Larsen (1956 World Series MVP) and Bob Turley (1958 WS MVP).

76. A—Bob Grim. Grim posted a 20–6 record with a 3.26 ERA in 1954.

77. B—Eddie Lopat. "Steady" Eddie posted an 80–36 record during the five-year stretch.

78. Elston Howard. Howard's debut for the Yankees came eight years after Jackie Robinson had broken Major League Baseball's color barrier in 1947.

79. A—Hank Bauer. Bauer was a member of seven World Series–winning teams with the Yankees from 1948 to 1959. The World Series hitting streak began in Game One of the 1956 World Series against the Brooklyn Dodgers and continued through the 1957 and 1958 World Series against the Milwaukee Braves, ending in Game Four in 1958.

80. A—Chairman of the Board. The moniker fit Ford's role as ace of the pitching staff.

81. D—Bobby Richardson. Freddie Freeman (Dodgers, 2024) equaled Richardson's mark of 12 RBIs in a Series.

82. Joe McCarthy. McCarthy won all seven titles with the Yankees, too.

83. Roger Maris. Maris hit a total of 100 home runs with 253 RBIs in those two seasons.

84. D—Tracy Stallard. Ironically, Maris's homer was the only run Stallard allowed in the game, which the Yankees won 1–0 over the Boston Red Sox on October 1, 1961.

85. Whitey Ford. Ford was 25–4 in 1961, and was dominant in the World Series, winning both his starts against the Cincinnati Reds and throwing 14 scoreless innings, including a shutout in Game One.

86. C—Billy Crystal. The film (*61**), which first aired on HBO in 2001, starred Barry Pepper as Roger Maris and Thomas Jane as Mickey Mantle on their quest to break Babe Ruth's 1927 single-season home run record of 60 during the 1961 season.

87. Ralph Houk. Known as "The Major," Houk managed the Yankees for 11 seasons, from 1961–63 and 1966–1973.

88. D—Barney Schultz. Mantle slammed the first pitch of the bottom of the ninth inning out of Yankee Stadium, giving New York a dramatic 2–1 walk-off victory and a two-games-to-one advantage over St. Louis.

89. Babe Ruth. Yogi Berra is third with 12 World Series homers.

90. Mel Allen. Allen was the announcer for the Yankees from 1940 through 1964.

91. C—Hoyt Wilhelm. Wilhelm, used almost exclusively as a reliever, no-hit the Yankees, 1–0, in his first career complete game at Baltimore's Memorial Stadium on September 20, 1958.

92. B—Elston Howard. Howard became the first African American player in American League history to win the honor.

93. B—The Commerce Comet. Mantle's nickname is derived from the city, Commerce, Oklahoma, where he grew up, and because he was an extremely fast runner.

94. A—Stan Bahnsen. Bahnsen was 17–12 with a 2.05 ERA in 1968.

95. Jim Bouton. Bouton was a member of the 1962 World Series team. He won 21 games in 1963 and 18 in 1964. The controversy surrounding the tell-all book stemmed from its unvarnished, inside look at major league baseball, which revealed the players' off-field behavior and violated their unwritten clubhouse code of silence.

96. Whitey Ford. Ford wore number 19 during his rookie season in 1950. He served in the Army from 1951 to 1952 during the Korean War. When he rejoined the Yankees for the 1953 season, he was assigned number 16, which he wore for the remainder of his Hall of Fame career. Ford's uniform number 16 was retired on Old Timers' Day in August 1974. He led the American League in victories three times, and in ERA and shutouts twice. He still holds several World Series records, including most wins (10) and strikeouts (94).

THE BRONX ZOO

QUESTIONS

The 1970s was an era of New York Yankees history defined by a chaotic and successful resurgence, transforming the team from a period of mediocrity in the late 1960s into a new championship dynasty. The transformation began when George Steinbrenner purchased the team in 1973, and aggressively utilized free agency to acquire star players with outsized personalities, like Catfish Hunter and Reggie Jackson. This star power, combined with the home-grown talents of catcher Thurman Munson and pitcher Ron Guidry, fueled a dramatic return to glory for the franchise. The decade also marked what became known as the "Bronx Zoo," the title of a tell-all book by pitcher Sparky Lyle that documented the turbulent dynamic between Steinbrenner, Jackson, and manager Billy Martin. Despite the rampant clubhouse conflicts that brought intense media attention, the Yankees achieved three consecutive American League pennants, from 1976 to 1978, and back-to-back World Series championships in 1977 and '78. The Yankees were once again The Boss of baseball.

97. Name the television network that sold the New York Yankees to a group headed by George Steinbrenner for a reported $10 million in January 1973.
Answer on page 51.

98. Which Yankees pitchers once exchanged wives, kids, and pets?
A. Jack Aker and Steve Kline
B. Al Closter and Ron Klimkowski
C. Doc Medich and Fred Beene
D. Fritz Peterson and Mike Kekich
Answer on page 51.

99. Lou Piniella was an outfielder on two World Series championship teams with the Yankees in the 1970s. Name the team for which he played when he was elected the 1969 American League Rookie of the Year.
Answer on page 51.

100. True or False. The Yankees played home games at Shea Stadium during the 1974 and 1975 seasons due to renovations of the original Yankee Stadium.
Answer on page 51.

101. Name the Yankee who won the 1970 American League Rookie of the Year Award and the 1976 American League Most Valuable Player Award.
Answer on page 51.

102. Which Yankees infielder hit the last grand slam at the original Yankee Stadium on September 8, 1973?
A. Horace Clarke
B. Jake Gibbs
C. Jim Mason
D. Fred Stanley
Answer on page 52.

103. Name the Oakland Athletics pitcher who won the 1974 American League Cy Young Award and two months later signed a five-year, $3.25 million free agent contract with the Yankees.
Answer on page 52.

104. Name the outfielder who became the first Yankee to record a 30-homer, 30-stolen base season in 1975, his only season with the team.
Answer on page 52.

105. The Yankees opened the remodeled Yankee Stadium with an 11–4 win over the Minnesota Twins on April 15, 1976. Name the visiting player who hit the first home run in the remodeled stadium.
A. Steve Braun
B. Steve Brye
C. Dan Ford
D. Larry Hisle
Answer on page 52.

106. Name the Kansas City Royals reliever who surrendered Chris Chambliss's ninth-inning home run in Game Five of the 1976 American League Championship Series to give the Yankees their 30th pennant.
Answer on page 52.

107. Which Yankees infielder hit a home run against the Cincinnati Reds in Game Three of the 1976 World Series in his only career World Series at-bat?
A. Sandy Alomar
B. Jim Mason
C. Willie Randolph
D. Fred Stanley
Answer on page 52.

108. Name the free agent signee who in spring training prior to the 1977 season created a sensation by proclaiming himself "the straw that stirs the drink."
Answer on page 52.

109. Reggie Jackson hit three home runs for the Yankees in the clinching Game Six of the 1977 World Series, hitting the first two homers off Los Angeles Dodgers pitchers Burt Hooton and Elias Sosa. Name the third Dodgers pitcher.
Answer on page 52.

110. Name the Yankees pitcher who in 1977 became the first reliever to win the American League Cy Young Award.
Answer on page 52.

111. Following the free agent signing of All-Star relief pitcher Rich Gossage prior to the 1978 season, which teammate joked that Sparky Lyle "went from Cy Young to Sayonara?"

A. Jay Johnstone
B. Andy Messersmith
C. Graig Nettles
D. Lou Piniella

Answer on page 52.

112. What was the nickname given to pitcher Rich Gossage?

Answer on page 53.

113. Name the Yankees television and radio broadcaster during this era whose much-spoken line was "Holy Cow!"

Answer on page 53.

114. Ron Guidry lost only three games during his 1978 Cy Young Award–winning season, and all three opposing pitchers who beat him were named Mike, including Mike Flanagan and Mike Willis. Who was the other Mike?

A. Mike Caldwell
B. Mike Marshall
C. Mike Norris
D. Mike Torrez

Answer on page 53.

115. Ron Guidry was born in Lafayette, Louisiana, which inspired two nicknames. One moniker was Gator. What was his other nickname?

Answer on page 53.

116. Name the Yankees manager who assumed the managerial role in the middle of the 1978 season and guided the team to a World Series title.
Answer on page 53.

117. Name the Boston Red Sox pitcher who surrendered a pivotal home run to Bucky Dent in the 1978 American League East Division tiebreaker game.
Answer on page 53.

118. Which Yankees television broadcaster made this iconic call on October 2, 1978? "Deep to left . . . Yastrzemski will not get it . . . it's a home run! A three-run home run for Bucky Dent and the Yankees now lead it by a score of 3 to 2."
A. Bob Gamere
B. Frank Messer
C. Phil Rizzuto
D. Bill White
Answer on page 53.

119. Which Los Angeles Dodgers pitcher dramatically struck out Reggie Jackson in an epic nine-pitch at bat in the ninth inning with two outs and the tying and go-ahead runs on base to close out the Dodgers' win in Game Two of the 1978 World Series?
A. Terry Forster
B. Rick Rhoden
C. Dave Stewart
D. Bob Welch
Answer on page 53.

120. Which Yankees infielder replaced an injured Willie Randolph at second base during the 1978 World Series triumph over the Los Angeles Dodgers?

A. Sandy Alomar
B. Brian Doyle
C. Damaso Garcia
D. George Zeber

Answer on page 53.

121. Which Los Angeles Dodgers infielder hit a foul popup that catcher Thurman Munson caught for the final out of the 1978 World Series?

A. Ron Cey
B. Bill Russell
C. Steve Garvey
D. Davey Lopes

Answer on page 53.

122. Name the Yankees player who won the 1978 World Series Most Valuable Player Award.

Answer on page 53.

123. Name the former Yankee who retired after a 22-year career in 1988 as the American League record holder for most career home runs by a third baseman.

Answer on page 54.

124. Which Yankees manager led the team to 103 victories in 1980, his only season in that role?

A. Yogi Berra
B. Dick Howser
C. Clyde King
D. Gene Michael

Answer on page 54.

125. Name the Yankees slugger who was known as Mr. October.
Answer on page 54.

126. How many stints did Billy Martin have as Yankees manager between 1975 and 1988?
Answer on page 54.

THE BRONX ZOO

ANSWERS

97. Columbia Broadcasting System. CBS had owned the team since 1964 and had presided over a 15-year pennant drought before concluding that sports franchises are more successful when owned by individuals rather than corporations.

98. D—Fritz Peterson and Mike Kekich. In a bizarre trade announced in March 1973, the pitchers literally swapped lives.

99. Kansas City Royals. The Yankees traded Lindy McDaniel to KC in exchange for Piniella on December 7, 1973. "Sweet Lou" played 11 seasons with the Yankees, won two World Series titles (1977 and '78), and later became the team's manager after his playing days.

100. True. The Yankees had a winning record of 172–150 during their two-season stay in Queens.

101. Thurman Munson. A catcher considered the heart and soul of the team, Munson was the Yankees' captain from 1976 until his death in a plane crash on August 2, 1979, devastating the franchise and its fans.

102. D—Fred Stanley. "Chicken" Stanley, a light-hitting shortstop who hit only 10 career homers, connected with a 3-2 curveball off Milwaukee's Kevin Kobel.

103. Jim "Catfish" Hunter. Hunter led the AL in wins (23), complete games (30), and innings pitched (328) in his first season in New York in 1975.

104. Bobby Bonds. Bonds hit 32 home runs with 30 stolen bases in 1975.

105. C—Dan Ford. "Disco" Dan Ford hit a two-run homer in the first inning off Yankees pitcher Rudy May.

106. Mark Littell. Chambliss hit Littell's first pitch for a game-ending home run over the right-field fence at Yankee Stadium on October 14, 1976, giving the Yankees a 7–6 victory and securing their first trip to the World Series since 1964.

107. B—Jim Mason. Mason homered off Cincinnati's Pat Zachry in the seventh inning of a 6–2 Yankees loss.

108. Reggie Jackson. In the June 1977 issue of *Sport* magazine, reporter Robert Ward quoted Jackson as saying, "I'm the straw that stirs the drink. Munson thinks he can be the straw, but he can only stir it bad." Jackson has consistently denied the quote, claiming the reporter fabricated it, which Ward has denied.

109. Charlie Hough. Jackson hit three home runs in the game off three different pitchers, all on the first pitch. He hit a total of five homers in the series.

110. Sparky Lyle. In 1977, Lyle went 13–5 with 26 saves and a 2.17 ERA for the eventual champs.

111. C—Graig Nettles. Nettles also famously quipped: "When I was a little boy, I wanted to be a baseball player and join the circus. With the Yankees I have accomplished both."

112. Goose. Gossage earned the nickname because of the way he would stick his neck out when getting signs from the catcher.

113. Phil Rizzuto. After his playing days, Rizzuto had a 40-year broadcasting career with the Yankees from 1956 to 1996.

114. A—Mike Caldwell. Caldwell went 22–9 with a 2.36 ERA in 1978 and finished second in the voting to Guidry for the American League Cy Young Award.

115. Louisiana Lightning. The nickname was given to him by announcer Phil Rizzuto to describe Guidry's blazing fastball.

116. Bob Lemon. Lemon took over after Billy Martin resigned on July 24, 1978.

117. Mike Torrez. The Yankees trailed 2–0 in the seventh inning when Dent belted a go-ahead three-run homer over the Green Monster off Torrez. The Yanks held on for a 5–4 win.

118. D—Bill White. A former player, White was later the president of the National League from 1989 to 1994.

119. D—Bob Welch. Welch went on to win the 1990 American League Cy Young Award while pitching for the Oakland Athletics.

120. B—Brian Doyle. Doyle batted .438 with seven hits, two RBIs, and four runs scored.

121. A—Ron Cey. The Yankees clinched the Series by winning Game Six 7–2 at Dodger Stadium. Rich Gossage pitched two innings of scoreless relief, retiring the Dodgers third baseman Ron Cey for the final out.

122. Bucky Dent. Dent batted .417 with 10 hits and seven RBIs in the Series.

123. Graig Nettles. Nettles hit 319 of his 390 career home runs in the American League. Mike Schmidt is the major league record-holder for homers among third basemen; Adrian Beltre is now the AL leader.

124. B—Dick Howser. Howser was fired after losing the 1980 American League Championship Series to the Kansas City Royals. He was hired by the Royals and managed the team to their first World Series title in 1985.

125. Reggie Jackson. Jackson earned the nickname for his prodigious postseason performance.

126. Five. Martin's tumultuous relationship with owner George Steinbrenner was characterized by frequent hirings and firings, fueled by their clashing egos and fiery personalities.

THE CORE FOUR

QUESTIONS

The Core Four era of New York Yankees history refers to a remarkable period of sustained excellence defined by four homegrown players who emerged through the team's minor league farm system in the mid-1990s and became the backbone of a new dynasty. Comprised of shortstop Derek Jeter, closer Mariano Rivera, catcher Jorge Posada, and pitcher Andy Pettitte, these four core players made their major league debuts in 1995, and were key contributors to the Yankees winning four World Series championship in five years, in 1996, 1998, 1999, and 2000, and a fifth title in 2009. Jeter, Rivera, and Posada played together for an impressive 17 consecutive seasons, a record for teammates in North American professional sports. Renowned for their consistency, clutch performance, and leadership, the homegrown quartet helped reestablish the Yankees as baseball's premier franchise for a new generation. All four players have had their numbers retired by the Yankees, and Rivera and Jeter were elected to the National Baseball Hall of Fame in 2019 and 2020, respectively. RE2PECT.

127. Which player was traded to the Cincinnati Reds prior to the 1993 season in exchange for outfielder Paul O'Neill?
A. Mel Hall
B. Dion James
C. Roberto Kelly
D. Danny Tartabull
Answer on page 65.

128. Which was the *Daily News* headline on November 3, 1995, announcing Joe Torre as new Yankees manager?
A. Clueless Joe
B. Gee, I Joe
C. Joe? Say It Ain't So
D. Trader Joe
Answer on page 65.

129. Derek Jeter hit a home run in his first at-bat in Cleveland on Opening Day of his rookie season on April 2, 1996. Which pitcher surrendered Jeter's first home run?
A. Orel Hershiser
B. Dennis Martínez
C. Jack McDowell
D. Charles Nagy
Answer on page 65.

130. Andy Pettitte of the Yankees finished in second place in balloting for the 1996 American League Cy Young Award. Which pitcher finished first in the voting?
A. Pat Hentgen
B. Mike Mussina
C. Charles Nagy
D. Mariano Rivera
Answer on page 65.

131. Which of these people was the twelve-year-old fan who assisted Derek Jeter's home run which tied the score in Game One of the 1996 American League Championship Series against the Baltimore Orioles?

A. Armando Benítez
B. Richie Garcia
C. Jeffrey Maier
D. Tony Tarasco

Answer on page 65.

132. Which Yankees player hit two home runs in Game Four of the 1996 American League Championship Series at Baltimore's Oriole Park at Camden Yards?

A. Wade Boggs
B. Jim Leyritz
C. Tim Raines
D. Darryl Strawberry

Answer on page 65.

133. Which Atlanta Braves pitcher surrendered a pivotal three-run home run to Jim Leyritz in the eighth inning of Game Four of the 1996 World Series?

A. Mike Bielecki
B. Denny Neagle
C. John Smoltz
D. Mark Wohlers

Answer on page 65.

134. Which Yankees infielder caught Mark Lemke's foul pop up for the final out of the 1996 World Series?
A. Wade Boggs
B. Mariano Duncan
C. Charlie Hayes
D. Chuck Knoblauch
Answer on page 65.

135. Which Yankees pitcher was the winning pitcher of the clinching Game Six of the 1996 World Series?
A. David Cone
B. Jimmy Key
C. Jeff Nelson
D. Kenny Rogers
Answer on page 66.

136. Name the Yankees player who famously celebrated the 1996 World Series triumph by riding off the field on a police horse.
Answer on page 66.

137. Which Yankees player won the 1996 World Series Most Valuable Player Award?
A. Derek Jeter
B. Paul O'Neill
C. Andy Pettitte
D. John Wetteland
Answer on page 66.

138. Which Yankees relief pitcher in 1996 became the first Australian-born player to win a World Series?

A. Darren Holmes
B. Graeme Lloyd
C. Scott Proctor
D. Tanyon Sturtze

Answer on page 66.

139. What song blaring over the Yankee Stadium loudspeaker spelled doom for opposing teams when Mariano Rivera entered a game?

Answer on page 66.

140. How many games did the 1998 Yankees win in the regular season?

A. 111
B. 114
C. 118
D. 125

Answer on page 66.

141. Which player joined the Yankees in September 1998 and proceeded to hit 10 home runs, including three grand slams, in just 67 regular season at-bats?

A. Homer Bush
B. Chad Curtis
C. Shane Spencer
D. Darryl Strawberry

Answer on page 66.

142. Name the Yankees pitcher who won an American League–leading 20 games in 1998, two seasons after surgery to treat an aneurysm in his shoulder.
Answer on page 66.

143. Who was the only pitcher on the 1998 Yankees to lose more than 10 games that season?
A. Hideki Irabu
B. Ramiro Mendoza
C. Andy Pettitte
D. David Wells
Answer on page 66.

144. Which Yankees player hit a go-ahead grand slam in Game One of the 1998 World Series off San Diego's Mark Langston?
A. Scott Brosius
B. Chuck Knoblauch
C. Tino Martinez
D. Paul O'Neill
Answer on page 66.

145. Which player was the Yankees rookie who went 6-for-10 with three doubles and four runs batted in during the 1998 World Series?
A. Ricky Ledée
B. Mike Lowell
C. Jorge Posada
D. Shane Spencer
Answer on page 66.

146. Which Cuban-born pitcher was known as El Duque?
A. Aroldis Chapman
B. Nestor Cortes
C. Orlando Hernández
D. Luis Tiant
Answer on page 67.

147. Which Yankees outfielder hit two home runs, including the walk-off homer, in Game Three of the 1999 World Series against the Atlanta Braves?
A. Chad Curtis
B. Glenallen Hill
C. David Justice
D. Chuck Knoblauch
Answer on page 67.

148. Which Yankees player won the 1999 World Series Most Valuable Player Award?
A. Derek Jeter
B. Andy Pettitte
C. Jorge Posada
D. Mariano Rivera
Answer on page 67.

149. On April 23, 2000, Jorge Posada and another Yankees switch-hitter became the first teammates in Major League Baseball history to homer from both sides of the plate in the same game. Who was that other switch-hitting teammate?
A. Melky Cabrera
B. Nick Swisher
C. Mark Teixeira
D. Bernie Williams
Answer on page 67.

150. What did Derek Jeter accomplish during the 2000 season that no player in major league history had ever accomplished?
A. Won AL MVP and World Series MVP
B. Won Rookie of the Year and World Series MVP
C. Won All-Star Game MVP and World Series MVP
D. Won Rookie of the Year and All-Star Game MVP
Answer on page 67.

151. Whose solo home run propelled the Yankees to a 1–0 victory in Game Three of the 2001 American League Division Series against the Oakland Athletics?
A. Clay Bellinger
B. David Justice
C. Tino Martinez
D. Jorge Posada
Answer on page 67.

152. Name the Arizona Diamondbacks batter who blooped a World Series–winning single off Mariano Rivera in the bottom of the ninth inning of Game Seven on November 4, 2001.
Answer on page 67.

153. Derek Jeter finished second in the voting for the 2006 American League Most Valuable Player Award. Which player won the award that season?
A. Vladimir Guerrero
B. Justin Morneau
C. David Ortiz
D. Ichiro Suzuki
Answer on page 68.

154. Which player hit the first regular-season home run at the current Yankee Stadium in 2009?

A. Brett Gardner
B. Chase Headley
C. Derek Jeter
D. Jorge Posada

Answer on page 68.

155. When Derek Jeter singled off Baltimore's Chris Tillman for career hit number 2,722 on September 11, 2009, he became the Yankees' all-time hits leader. Which Yankee did he surpass?

A. Joe DiMaggio
B. Lou Gehrig
C. Mickey Mantle
D. Babe Ruth

Answer on page 68.

156. Jorge Posada finished his career with 275 home runs, the most ever by a switch-hitting catcher. Who is second on that list?

A. Victor Martínez
B. Ted Simmons
C. Mickey Tettleton
D. Jason Varitek

Answer on page 68.

157. What did Mariano Rivera do for the first time in his career in the 2009 game against the New York Mets when he earned his 500th career save?

A. First balk committed
B. First grand slam allowed
C. First immaculate inning achieved
D. First run batted in

Answer on page 68.

158. What was the outcome of Derek Jeter's final career at-bat at Yankee Stadium in a game against the Baltimore Orioles on September 25, 2014?

A. Foul pop out
B. Inside the park home run
C. Intentional walk
D. Walk-off hit

Answer on page 68.

159. Who finished his career as the first player to pitch more than 15 major league seasons without ever having a losing record?

A. Roger Clemens
B. Whitey Ford
C. Randy Johnson
D. Andy Pettitte

Answer on page 68.

THE CORE FOUR

ANSWERS

127. C—Roberto Kelly. Kelly was an All-Star for the Yankees in 1992, a season in which he hit 31 doubles and stole 28 bases.

128. A—Clueless Joe. The headline's skepticism was based on Torre's previous managerial record which had limited success.

129. B—Dennis Martínez. Jeter hit 260 home runs during his 20-year career all with the Yankees.

130. A—Pat Hentgen. Rivera finished third, Nagy was fourth, and Mussina fifth.

131. C—Jeffrey Maier. Maier reached over the fence and prevented Baltimore outfielder Tony Tarasco from grabbing Jeter's eighth-inning drive off pitcher Armando Benítez. Umpire Richie Garcia did not call fan interference.

132. D—Darryl Strawberry. Straw was 3-for-4 with three RBIs in the Yankees' 8–4 victory.

133. D—Mark Wohlers. Leyritz's homer tied the score 6–6. The Yankees went on to win the game in extra innings, tying the Series.

134. C—Charlie Hayes.

135. B—Jimmy Key. Key pitched 5 1/3 innings of one-run ball in his last start as a member of the Yankees.

136. Wade Boggs. Boggs won his only World Series title with the Yankees in 1996, famously drawing a bases-loaded walk in the 10th inning of Game Four to drive in the go-ahead run.

137. D—John Wetteland. Wetteland saved all four Yankees victories in the series.

138. B—Graeme Lloyd. A native of Victoria, Australia, Lloyd was a member of the Yankees title teams in 1996 and 1998.

139. Metallica's "Enter Sandman." The Yankees used the iconic walk-out song for Rivera from 1999 until his retirement in 2013 to generate excitement for the closer's entrance. Rivera was not the one who chose it but grew to appreciate the song that became synonymous with his legendary career.

140. B—114. The '98 Yanks dominated their way to 114 regular season wins, which at the time was the most in MLB history. In total, the Bombers won 125 games, including the postseason.

141. C—Shane Spencer. Spencer hit two more homers in the Division Series against the Texas Rangers.

142. David Cone. Cone finished fourth in the Cy Young Award voting in 1998. He won the award with Kansas City in 1994.

143. C—Andy Pettitte. Pettitte's record was 16–11 in 1998.

144. C—Tino Martinez. The Yankees won the opening game, 9–6, and the Padres would eventually get swept in the Series.

145. A—Ricky Ledée. Ledée reached base in his first seven plate appearances in the 1998 World Series. He was also a part of the Yankees' championship team in 1999.

146. C—Orlando Hernández. El Duque joined the Yankees in 1998 and was a key part of the team's three-peat, from 1998 to 2000. He won a fourth World Series ring with the Chicago White Sox in 2005.

147. A—Chad Curtis. Curtis led off the 10th inning and hit a home run off Atlanta's Mike Remlinger to give the Yankees a 3–0 series lead.

148. D—Mariano Rivera. Rivera allowed no runs in 4 2/3 innings pitched. He had saves in Games One and Four and earned the win in Game Three as the Yankees swept the Braves to win their 25th World Championship.

149. D—Bernie Williams. Williams and Posada each homered batting left-handed off Toronto's Frank Castillo and batting right-handed off Clayton Andrews.

150. C—Won All-Star Game MVP and World Series MVP. Jeter went 3-for-3 with a double and a two-run single in the All-Star Game played in Atlanta to become the first Yankee to win the award. In the five-game World Series he had nine hits and six runs scored. He batted .409 with two doubles, a triple, two home runs, two RBIs, 19 total bases, and three walks.

151. D—Jorge Posada. Down 0–2 in the best-of-five series and facing elimination, Posada hit a solo home run off Athletics pitcher Barry Zito in the top of the fifth inning, which proved to be the only run of the game.

152. Luis Gonzalez. Gonzalez's single ended New York's bid for a fourth consecutive title (and fifth in six seasons) and brought Arizona its first championship in its fourth year of existence, making the Diamondbacks the fastest expansion team to win a World Series.

153. B—Justin Morneau. In a tight race, Minnesota Twins first baseman Morneau received 15 first place votes to Jeter's 12.

154. D—Jorge Posada. Posada connected in the fifth inning off Cleveland's Cliff Lee in a 10–2 loss on April 16, 2009.

155. B—Lou Gehrig. With 2,721 hits, Gehrig had stood as the Yankees' all-time hits leader for more than seventy years.

156. B—Ted Simmons. Simmons hit 248 homers during his 21-year career mostly with the St. Louis Cardinals, Milwaukee Brewers, and Atlanta Braves from 1968 to 1988.

157. D—First run batted in. Rivera walked with the bases loaded, earning his first career RBI against the Mets on June 28, 2009.

158. D—Walk-off hit. With the game tied 5–5 in the bottom of the ninth, Jeter hit an opposite-field single on the first pitch that scored Antoan Richardson for the winning run.

159. D—Andy Pettitte. Pettitte's career mark was 256–153 for a .626 winning percentage over his 18-year career with the Yankees and Houston Astros.

LEGENDARY MOMENTS

QUESTIONS

From the deafening roar of Babe Ruth's "Called Shot" to the quiet dignity of Derek Jeter's farewell tour, the storied history of the New York Yankees is not merely a chronicle of wins and losses, but a vibrant tapestry woven with legendary, indelible moments that transcend the sport itself. This chapter delves into the pivotal events that eclipse mere statistics; indeed, these significant events have defined baseball's most iconic franchise. We will revisit the high-stakes drama of Don Larsen's perfect game in the World Series, the unparalleled achievement of Reggie Jackson's three home runs in a single Fall Classic contest, and Aaron Boone's iconic walk-off home run in the League Championship Series, to name a few instances that are the pinnacle of individual brilliance on the grandest stage. These dramatic moments are the snapshots in time that are etched into the collective memory of generations of fans, and that forged the Yankees' legacy and enduring mythology.

160. Which Yankees slugger was the first player of the modern era to hit four home runs in one game?
A. Lou Gehrig
B. Mickey Mantle
C. Johnny Mize
D. Babe Ruth
Answer on page 77.

161. Which Yankees player hit the first home run in All-Star Game history?
A. Frank Crosetti
B. Bill Dickey
C. Lou Gehrig
D. Babe Ruth
Answer on page 77.

162. Name the Brooklyn Dodgers pinch-hitter who made the final out of Don Larsen's perfect game in Game Five of the 1956 World Series.
Answer on page 77.

163. Which Yankees player hit two home runs in one inning against the Kansas City Athletics on May 23, 1962?
A. Clete Boyer
B. Elston Howard
C. Héctor López
D. Joe Pepitone
Answer on page 77.

164. Which Yankees player hit a two-run home run in the 22nd inning to end the longest game in Yankees history on June 24, 1962?
A. Bob Cerv
B. Jake Gibbs
C. Héctor López
D. Jack Reed
Answer on page 77.

165. Name the Yankees pitcher who threw a no-hitter against the Boston Red Sox at Yankee Stadium on July 4, 1983.
Answer on page 77.

166. Name the Yankees pitcher who surrendered a home run to Kansas City's George Brett in the infamous Pine Tar Game against the Royals at Yankee Stadium on July 24, 1983.
Answer on page 78.

167. Name the future Hall of Fame pitcher who won his 300th career game at Yankee Stadium on Phil Rizzuto Day on August 3, 1985.
A. Ted Lyons
B. Tom Seaver
C. Hoyt Wilhelm
D. Early Wynn
Answer on page 78.

168. Name the Yankees left-handed pitcher who threw a no-hitter against the Cleveland Indians at Yankee Stadium on September 4, 1993.
Answer on page 78.

169. Which Yankees batter hit the walk-off home run off Seattle's Tim Belcher in the 15th inning to win Game Two of the 1995 American League Division Series?
A. Jim Leyritz
B. Rubén Sierra
C. Luis Sojo
D. Bernie Williams
Answer on page 78.

170. Name the Yankees pitcher who thew a no-hitter against the Seattle Mariners at Yankee Stadium on May 14, 1996.
Answer on page 78.

171. Which Yankees pitcher threw the only perfect game ever caught by Jorge Posada?
A. David Cone
B. Domingo Germán
C. Don Larsen
D. David Wells
Answer on page 78.

172. Which Yankees player caught the final out of David Cone's perfect game in 1999?
A. Scott Brosius
B. Joe Girardi
C. Ricky Ledée
D. Paul O'Neill
Answer on page 78.

173. Name the Oakland Athletics baserunner who was tagged out at home plate when Derek Jeter made the iconic Flip Play during Game Three of the 2001 American League Division Series.
Answer on page 79.

174. Which Yankees player hit the game-tying home run off Arizona's Byung-Hyun Kim in the ninth inning of Game Four of the 2001 World Series?
A. Nick Johnson
B. David Justice
C. Chuck Knoblauch
D. Tino Martinez
Answer on page 79.

175. Which Yankees rookie hit a home run facing the future Hall of Fame pitcher Randy Johnson in his first major league baseball at-bat?
A. Drew Henson
B. Nick Johnson
C. Marcus Thames
D. Shane Spencer
Answer on page 79.

176. Name the pitcher who struck out the 4,000th batter of his career on the same night he won his 300th game at Yankee Stadium on June 13, 2003.
Answer on page 79.

177. Name the Boston Red Sox pitcher who surrendered Aaron Boone's walk-off home run in Game Seven of the 2003 American League Championship Series.
Answer on page 79.

178. Name the Yankees slugger who hit a three-run home run and a grand slam in the sixth inning of the 2009 season finale at Tampa Bay, setting an all-time American League mark with seven RBIs in an inning.
Answer on page 79.

179. Name the Yankees outfielder who equaled a World Series single-game record by driving in six runs in the deciding Game Six of the 2009 World Series.
Answer on page 79.

180. Name the Tampa Bay Rays pitcher who surrendered a home run to Derek Jeter for The Captain's 3,000th career hit on July 9, 2011.
Answer on page 79.

181. On August 25, 2011, the Yankees became the first team in MLB history to hit three grand slams in one game. The homers were hit by Curtis Granderson, Robinson Canó, and which additional player?
A. Brett Gardner
B. Russell Martin
C. Nick Swisher
D. Mark Teixeira
Answer on page 80.

182. Which Yankees pitcher hurled a complete game against the Baltimore Orioles in Game Five of the 2012 American League Division Series to clinch the Series victory?
A. Phil Hughes
B. CC Sabathia
C. Andy Pettitte
D. Hiroki Kuroda
Answer on page 80.

183. Which Yankees relief pitcher was the first reliever to be selected as the All-Star Game Most Valuable Player?
A. Aroldis Chapman
B. Jeff Reardon
C. Mariano Rivera
D. Lee Smith
Answer on page 80.

184. Which pitcher surrendered a home run to Álex Rodríguez for the slugger's 3,000th career hit?
A. Corey Kluber
B. Rick Porcello
C. Chris Sale
D. Justin Verlander
Answer on page 80.

185. Which pitcher threw the first Yankees no-hitter of the twenty-first century?
A. Corey Kluber
B. Domingo Germán
C. Gerrit Cole
D. Luis Severino
Answer on page 80.

186. Name the Yankees pitcher who achieved the 24th perfect game in major league history against the Oakland Athletics on June 28, 2023.
Answer on page 80.

187. Which Texas Rangers pitcher surrendered Aaron Judge's American League record-setting 62nd home run, at Globe Life Field in Arlington, Texas on October 4, 2022?

A. Jon Gray
B. José Leclerc
C. Josh Sborz
D. Jesús Tinoco

Answer on page 80.

LEGENDARY MOMENTS

ANSWERS

160. A—Lou Gehrig. Gehrig hit four homers in the Yankees' 20–13 win over the Athletics at Philadelphia's Shibe Park on June 3, 1932.

161. D—Babe Ruth. The first All-Star Game was played in Chicago's Comiskey Park in 1933. The AL defeated the NL, 4–2. Ruth, who launched a two-run shot in the third inning, hit the first home run.

162. Dale Mitchell. Mitchell was called out on strikes by home-plate umpire Babe Pinelli.

163. D—Joe Pepitone. Pepitone hit two homers during an eighth-inning rally when the Yankees scored nine runs against the Kansas City Athletics on the way to a 13–7 victory.

164. D—Jack Reed. Reed's homer was the margin of victory in a 9–7 win at Detroit.

165. Dave Righetti. Righetti's no-hitter was the Yankees' first no-hitter since Don Larsen's perfect game in the 1956 World Series and the first by a Yankees left-hander since 1917. The final out was a swinging strikeout of future Hall of Famer Wade Boggs.

166. Goose Gossage. Brett homered off Gossage in the top of the ninth inning to give the Royals a 5–4 lead. But Yankees manager Billy Martin informed umpire Tim McClelland that Brett's bat was covered with more pine tar than the rule allowed. McClelland agreed that the bat violated the rule and signaled that Brett was out, ending the game. An enraged Brett charged out of the dugout to argue, but the call stood. Or so it seemed. The Royals protested and after league officials upheld the protest, the teams reconvened at Yankee Stadium on August 18 to resume the game from the point Brett had homered. Royals reliever Dan Quisenberry pitched a perfect bottom of the ninth to preserve Kansas City's 5–4 win.

167. B—Tom Seaver. This may be the only game when the Yankee Stadium crowd rooted against the home team.

168. Jim Abbott. Abbott was a successful major league pitcher despite being born without a right hand.

169. A—Jim Leyritz. Leyritz drove Belcher's 3-1 pitch high over the right-center field wall and ended the five-hour marathon game in dramatic walk-off fashion. In addition to the game having seven lead changes, it was significant in that it was Don Mattingly's last game at Yankee Stadium, and the winning pitcher was rookie reliever Mariano Rivera.

170. Dwight Gooden. Gooden threw 134 pitches, walked six batters, and struck out five on his way to a 2–0 win over Seattle.

171. D—David Wells. On May 17, 1998, Wells pitched the 15th perfect game in MLB history and the second in Yankees history, beating the Minnesota Twins, 4–0.

172. A—Scott Brosius. Montreal's Orlando Cabrera popped up to third baseman Brosius in foul territory to end the game on July 18, 1999.

173. Jeremy Giambi. Giambi was on first base with the Athletics trailing 1–0 in the seventh inning when Terrence Long laced a double off Mike Mussina to right fielder Shane Spencer, who fielded and threw the ball toward home plate. But Spencer overthrew the cutoff man, and the throw landed in no-man's land between first and home as Giambi charged around the bases. That's when Jeter sprinted to the bouncing ball and flipped it to catcher Jorge Posada like a shovel pass from a quarterback. Posada swiped the leg of Giambi in a bang-bang play at the plate. The umpire made the call. Giambi was out.

174. D—Tino Martinez. The Yankees won the game in extra innings but lost the Series in seven games.

175. C—Marcus Thames. Thames hit a home run on the first MLB pitch he saw from Arizona's Randy Johnson on June 10, 2002.

176. Roger Clemens. Clemens became the 21st pitcher to win 300 games, beating the St. Louis Cardinals 5–2. He recorded 10 strikeouts, including number 4,000 in the second inning, when he fanned Edgar Renteria on a high fastball.

177. Tim Wakefield. Boone homered off Wakefield's first pitch leading off the bottom of the 11th inning.

178. Álex Rodríguez. Rodríguez hit a three-run homer off Rays pitcher Wade Davis and a grand slam off Andy Sonnanstine in the Yankees' 10–2 victory.

179. Hideki Matsui. Matsui batted .615 with three HRs and eight RBIs to earn the World Series MVP Award.

180. David Price. Jeter became just the second player to record his 3,000th hit on a homer, following Wade Boggs, who accomplished the feat in 1999. Jeter would finish the game a perfect

5-for-5, with a double, three singles and a homer. His final hit of the day was an RBI single that game New York a 5–4 win.

181. B—Russell Martin. The Yankees fell behind 7–1 after three innings before routing the Oakland Athletics, 22–9.

182. B—CC Sabathia. Sabathia went the distance in the series-deciding game at Yankee Stadium, striking out nine Orioles while allowing one run and four hits.

183. C—Mariano Rivera. In 2013, Rivera became the first reliever in the eighty-four-year history of the All-Star Game to be named the MVP.

184. D—Justin Verlander. Rodríguez connected off Verlander at Yankee Stadium on June 19, 2015.

185. A—Corey Kluber. Kluber beat the Texas Rangers, 2–0, allowing only a third inning walk on May 19, 2021.

186. Domingo Germán. Germán pitched the fourth perfect game in Yankees franchise history, an 11–0 win against the Athletics at the Oakland Coliseum.

187. D—Jesús Tinoco. Tinoco grooved a slider at 88 miles per hour on the third pitch of Texas' 3–2 win, and Judge launched it 391 feet over the left-field wall.

NOTABLE RIVALRIES

QUESTIONS

The Yankees' rich history includes intense rivalries, the most famous and enduring with the Boston Red Sox—considered by many to be the fiercest in American sports. The Yankees-Red Sox feud intensified after the 1920 sale of Babe Ruth to the Yankees, which led to the "Curse of the Bambino" that lasted over eight decades until Boston's 2004 World Series win. Historically, the Yankees' rivalry with the Dodgers and Giants is also significant. Before the Dodgers moved to Los Angeles and Giants to San Francisco in 1958, the teams, both based in New York, faced each other multiple times in the World Series. Including their now East Coast vs. West Coast rivalry, the Yankees and Dodgers have met twelve times in the World Series—five more than any other two teams—with the Yankees winning eight times. The second-most frequent matchup was between the Yankees and their other once-upon-a-time crosstown rival, the Giants. The Yankees and Giants have met seven times for a championship, with the Yankees winning five times, though they last faced off in 1962. That Series is famous for its dramatic Game Seven conclusion, when Yankees second baseman Bobby Richardson made a game-saving catch off a line drive hit by the Giants' Willie McCovey with the winning runs on base in the bottom of the ninth inning. The World Series between the Yankees and Brooklyn Dodgers or New York Giants was called "The Subway Series," as fans could shuttle between the two ballparks using public transportation. The current Subway Series refers to the strong local rivalry with the New York Mets, thanks to interleague play. This rivalry pits New York's American League team (Yankees) against its National League counterpart (Mets), with bragging rights for the city at stake. Never more was this evident than when the two teams met in the 2000 World Series, which the Yankees won in five games. To a lesser extent, but no less important, the Yankees and their fans hold grudges against current rivals that include the Houston Astros, Baltimore Orioles, Seattle Mariners, Cleveland Guardians, Minnesota Twins, Philadelphia Phillies, and any other team that stands in their way of postseason success.

188. Which player hit the first World Series home run at the original Yankee Stadium in 1923?
A. Frank Crosetti
B. Leo Durocher
C. Casey Stengel
D. Bill Terry
Answer on page 89.

189. Which Yankees infielder made a game-saving running catch of a high infield popup hit by Brooklyn's Jackie Robinson with the bases loaded and two outs in the seventh inning of Game Seven of the 1952 World Series to help the Yankees secure their fourth consecutive championship?
A. Joe Collins
B. Billy Martin
C. Gil McDougald
D. Phil Rizzuto
Answer on page 89.

190. Which Yankees player set a World Series record with 13 hits in the 1964 World Series against the St. Louis Cardinals?

A. Clete Boyer
B. Roger Maris
C. Gil McDougald
D. Bobby Richardson

Answer on page 89.

191. Which Yankees pitcher set a World Series record by pitching 33 consecutive scoreless innings?

A. Whitey Ford
B. Lefty Gomez
C. Allie Reynolds
D. Red Ruffing

Answer on page 89.

192. Name the two starting pitchers for the Yankees and Los Angeles Dodgers in Game Three of the 1981 World Series. Hint: they were the American League and National League Rookies of the Year that season.

Answer on page 89.

193. Which Yankees pitcher equaled a World Series record by losing three games against the Los Angeles Dodgers in 1981?

A. Ron Davis
B. George Frazier
C. Dave LaRoche
D. Rudy May

Answer on page 90.

194. Two former New York Mets who were winners of the National League Rookie of the Year Award were then members of the Yankees' 1996 World Series–winning team. Darryl Strawberry was one. Name the other.
Answer on page 90.

195. Name the only Yankees player who has hit two postseason walk-off home runs.
Answer on page 90.

196. Name the Yankees batter who supplied the game-winning, walk-off hit with two outs in the bottom of the 12th inning to give the Yankees a 4–3 victory over the New York Mets in Game One of the 2000 World Series.
Answer on page 90.

197. Which New York Mets pitcher surrendered a leadoff home run to Derek Jeter on the first pitch of Game Four of the 2000 World Series?
A. Mike Hampton
B. Bobby Jones
C. Al Leiter
D. Rick Reed
Answer on page 90.

198. Name the Yankees batter who hit a ninth-inning single against the New York Mets to drive in the winning runs in the clinching Game Five of the 2000 World Series.
Answer on page 90.

199. Name the New York Mets pitcher who took the loss in the deciding Game Five of the 2000 World Series.
Answer on page 90.

200. Which relief pitcher earned two victories in the 2000 World Series against the New York Mets?
A. Jeff Nelson
B. Ramiro Mendoza
C. Mike Stanton
D. Randy Choate
Answer on page 90.

201. Who won the 2000 World Series Most Valuable Player Award?
A. Scott Brosius
B. Derek Jeter
C. Jorge Posada
D. Bernie Williams
Answer on page 90.

202. Which Yankees starting pitcher threw three shutout innings of relief against the Red Sox in Game Seven of the 2003 American League Championship Series?
A. Mike Mussina
B. Orlando Hernández
C. Andy Pettitte
D. David Wells
Answer on page 90.

203. Name the pitcher who threw a complete-game shutout against the Yankees in Game Six of the 2003 World Series to clinch the championship for the Florida Marlins.
Answer on page 90.

204. Select the former Yankees prospect that was voted the 2007 World Series Most Valuable Player Award as a member of the Boston Red Sox.
A. Josh Beckett
B. Mike Lowell
C. Dustin Pedroia
D. Hanley Ramírez
Answer on page 91.

205. Which Yankees pitcher won the 2009 American League Championship Series Most Valuable Player Award by dominating the Los Angeles Angels of Anaheim?
A. A. J. Burnett
B. Andy Pettitte
C. Mariano Rivera
D. CC Sabathia
Answer on page 91.

206. Which Philadelphia Phillie was the winning pitcher in Game One of the 2009 World Series, the first World Series game played in the new Yankee Stadium?
A. Cole Hamels
B. J.A. Happ
C. Cliff Lee
D. Ryan Madson
Answer on page 91.

207. Which Yankees player dared to steal two bases on one play during a pivotal ninth inning rally in Game Four of the 2009 World Series?

A. Melky Cabrera
B. Johnny Damon
C. Derek Jeter
D. Álex Rodríguez

Answer on page 91.

208. Which Yankees batter drove in six runs against the Detroit Tigers in Game One of the 2011 American League Division Series?

A. Robinson Canó
B. Brett Gardner
C. Russell Martin
D. Álex Rodríguez

Answer on page 91.

209. Which Yankees batter hit two dramatic home runs against the Baltimore Orioles, one in the ninth inning to tie the score and the other a walk-off in the 12th inning to win Game Three of the 2012 American League Division Series?

A. Eric Chavez
B. Curtis Granderson
C. Raúl Ibañez
D. Nick Swisher

Answer on page 91.

210. Which one of the following players earned a World Series ring as both a member of the Yankees and Red Sox?
A. Nathan Eovaldi
B. Eric Hinske
C. Doug Mientkiewicz
D. Kevin Youkilis
Answer on page 91.

211. Name the Yankees player who equaled the World Series single-game record by stealing three bases against the Los Angeles Dodgers in Game One of the 2024 World Series.
Answer on page 91.

212. Name the Yankees player who hit a grand slam against the Dodgers in Game Four of the 2024 World Series.
Answer on page 91.

NOTABLE RIVALRIES

ANSWERS

188. C—Casey Stengel. Stengel, then an outfielder for the New York Giants, broke a 4–4 tie in the top of the ninth inning with an inside-the-park home run off Yankees pitcher Joe Bush, giving the Giants a Game One victory in the first postseason game ever played at Yankee Stadium.

189. B—Billy Martin. First baseman Joe Collins appeared to lose the ball in the sun, but Martin, the second baseman, charged in from his position to make a lunging, shoetop catch just in front of the pitchers' mound. The catch snuffed out the Dodgers' last major threat, and the Yankees went on to win the game 4–2, clinching the World Series.

190. D—Bobby Richardson. Lou Brock (Cardinals, 1968) and Marty Barrett (Red Sox, 1986) equaled Richardson's mark of 13 hits in a single World Series.

191. A—Whitey Ford. Ford's record scoreless innings streak lasted from the 1960 to 1962 World Series.

192. Fernando Valenzuela and Dave Righetti. Valenzuela, the Game Three winning pitcher, was also the 1981 NL Cy Young Award winner.

193. B—George Frazier. Frazier tied the record for most losses in a World Series set by Lefty Williams in the infamous 1919 World Series.

194. Dwight Gooden. Gooden's rookie year was 1984, when the nineteen-year-old pitcher had a 17–9 record, a 2.60 ERA, and a major league–leading 276 strikeouts, breaking a rookie record at the time.

195. Bernie Williams. Williams hit walk-offs in Game One of the 1996 ALCS against Baltimore and Game One of the 1999 ALCS against Boston.

196. José Vizcaíno. Vizcaíno's single came with the bases loaded against Mets pitcher Turk Wendell.

197. B—Bobby Jones. The Yankees won the game 3–2 to take a three-games-to-one Series lead.

198. Luis Sojo. Sojo's series-clinching hit was a single that broke a 2–2 tie and propelled the Yankees to their third consecutive championship.

199. Al Leiter. The former Yankees left-hander pitched 8 2/3 innings, throwing 142 pitches before being removed from the game, won by the Yankees 4–2.

200. C—Mike Stanton. Stanton retired all 13 Mets batters he faced across four appearances.

201. B—Derek Jeter. Jeter batted .409 with nine hits and two home runs in the five-game Series victory over the Mets.

202. A—Mike Mussina. It was the first time Mussina came out of the bullpen during his 18-year career, from 1991 to 2008.

203. Josh Beckett. Beckett was named the World Series MVP for his performance in the series.

204. B—Mike Lowell. Lowell batted .400 with a home run and four RBIs in the Red Sox' sweep over the Colorado Rockies.

205. D—CC Sabathia. Sabathia won two games in the Series, allowing just two runs over 16 innings against the Angels.

206. C—Cliff Lee. Lee outdueled CC Sabathia in Game One, giving up only an unearned run in a complete game 6–1 victory.

207. B—Johnny Damon. By stealing two bases on one play, Damon set the stage for the tie-breaking three-run rally, giving the Yankees a 3–1 Series lead.

208. A—Robinson Canó. Canó tied the franchise postseason record for RBIs in a game by a single player.

209. C—Raúl Ibañez. Ibañez tied the score while pinch-hitting for Álex Rodríguez in the ninth inning, then hit a leadoff homer in the 12th, giving the Yankees a stunning 3–2 win over the Orioles for a 2–1 lead in the series.

210. B—Eric Hinske. Hinske won World Series titles with Boston in 2007 and New York in 2009.

211. Jazz Chisholm Jr. Chisholm's feat had been accomplished six times prior.

212. Anthony Volpe. Volpe connected off Dodgers right-hander Daniel Hudson in the third inning to give the Yankees a 5–2 lead. The Yankees went on to win the game 11–4 and avoid a sweep.

THE MODERN ERA

QUESTIONS

Thirty-eight members of the Yankees organization have been honored in Monument Park, while twenty-three have had their uniform numbers retired. The most recent is former ace pitcher CC Sabathia, a first-ballot honoree to the National Baseball Hall of Fame, who was immortalized among the game's greatest players, on July 27, 2025. Sabathia's next honor will be for his jersey retirement ceremony on September 26, 2026, and a spot beyond the center field wall at Yankee Stadium in Monument Park, where his legacy can be displayed next to the great Yankees in franchise history. The modern Yankees era (post-2001) has featured several high-impact players who might one day see their numbers retired and receive plaques in Monument Park. The most prominent current candidate is Aaron Judge, the team captain and three-time Most Valuable Player, who broke the American League single-season home run record with 62 in 2022. His blend of power, defense, and leadership makes his induction seem very likely, especially if he helps secure another World Series title after coming so close in 2024. After that, Gerritt Cole and several members of the current roster have a good chance to be recognized, but only time will tell.

213. In which year did the newest version of Yankee Stadium officially open?
A. 2001
B. 2009
C. 2011
D. 2019
Answer on page 101.

214. Which Yankee was the first player in Major League Baseball history to record 40 home runs, 10 triples, and 25 stolen bases in a single season in 2011?
A. Robinson Canó
B. Jacoby Ellsbury
C. Curtis Granderson
D. Álex Rodríguez
Answer on page 101.

215. Name the reigning National League Most Valuable Player who was traded to the Yankees in December 2017.
Answer on page 101.

216. Name the Yankees broadcaster that describes an Álex Rodríguez home run as being "an A-Bomb, from A-Rod."
A. Michael Kay
B. Bob Lorenz
C. Ryan Ruocco
D. John Sterling
Answer on page 101.

217. Which player was traded to the Yankees on June 29, 2000, and then went on to win the 2000 American League Championship Series Most Valuable Player Award against the Seattle Mariners?

A. David Justice
B. José Canseco
C. Chuck Knoblauch
D. Scott Brosius

Answer on page 101.

218. Which player represented five different teams including the Yankees in the All-Star Game, the most in All-Star Game history?

A. Carlos Beltrán
B. Reggie Jackson
C. Gary Sheffield
D. Dave Winfield

Answer on page 101.

219. Who signed a three-year, $21 million deal ahead of the 2003 season and then became the first Japanese-born player to hit a home run in the World Series?

Answer on page 101.

220. Which Yankees pitcher threw a near perfect game against the Red Sox at Boston's Fenway Park on September 2, 2001?

A. Roger Clemens
B. Orlando Hernández
C. Mike Mussina
D. Andy Pettitte

Answer on page 102.

221. Name the 2000 American League Most Valuable Player who signed a seven-year, $120 million contract with the Yankees in December 2001, and then slugged 41 home runs in both the 2002 and 2003 seasons.
Answer on page 102.

222. Hideki Matsui of the Yankees finished in second place in balloting for the 2003 American League Rookie of the Year Award. Who finished first in the voting?
A. Ángel Berroa
B. Rocco Baldelli
C. Jody Gerut
D. Mark Teixeira
Answer on page 102.

223. Who was the only closer other than Mariano Rivera to lead the Yankees in saves between 1997 and 2013?
Answer on page 102.

224. Mike Mussina recorded his 200th career victory on April 11, 2004. Which teammate secured his 200th career victory three days later?
A. Kevin Brown
B. José Contreras
C. Orlando Hernández
D. Javier Vázquez
Answer on page 102.

225. Which pitcher led the American League with 19 wins in 2006?
A. Tom Gordon
B. Randy Johnson
C. Mike Mussina
D. Chien-Ming Wang
Answer on page 102.

226. Name the team for which Joe Girardi was manager when he won the 2006 National League Manager of the Year Award.
Answer on page 102.

227. Which Hall of Fame pitcher retired at the top of his game, posting his only 20-win season in his final year as an active player?
A. Whitey Ford
B. Mike Mussina
C. Phil Niekro
D. Gaylord Perry
Answer on page 102.

228. True or False. Robinson Canó recorded more hits than any other player in the decade of the 2010s.
Answer on page 102.

229. Where did Aaron Judge play college baseball?
A. Fresno State
B. Pepperdine
C. Santa Clara
D. Southern California
Answer on page 102.

230. Aaron Judge and which teammate are the first players ever to make their Major League Baseball debut and hit back-to-back home runs in their first at bats?

A. Tyler Austin
B. Ben Gamel
C. Rob Refsnyder
D. Gary Sánchez

Answer on page 103.

231. Name the player who hit 33 home runs in 2017 to surpass the previous franchise record for catchers shared by Yogi Berra and Jorge Posada (30).

Answer on page 103.

232. Who broke Aaron Judge's single-season rookie home run record?

A. Ronald Acuña Jr.
B. Pete Alonso
C. Julio Rodríguez
D. Fernando Tatis Jr.

Answer on page 103.

233. Which Yankees player earned his second All-Star Game selection in 2019 before turning twenty-three years old?

A. Didi Gregorius
B. Aaron Judge
C. Gary Sánchez
D. Gleyber Torres

Answer on page 103.

234. Which Yankees slugger led the American League in home runs in 2020?

A. Luke Voit
B. DJ LeMahieu
C. Gary Sánchez
D. Aaron Judge

Answer on page 103.

235. Which player won batting titles in both the American and National Leagues?

A. Matt Holliday
B. DJ LeMahieu
C. Paul O'Neill
D. Gary Sheffield

Answer on page 103.

236. Name the Yankees player who won the 2022 All-Star Game Most Valuable Player Award.

Answer on page 103.

237. Who hit a home run on his first swing in a major league game on September 1, 2023?

A. Oswaldo Cabrera
B. Jasson Domínguez
C. Oswald Peraza
D. Austin Wells

Answer on page 103.

238. Who was the first Yankees rookie to win a Gold Glove Award?

A. Brett Gardner
B. Aaron Judge
C. Gleyber Torres
D. Anthony Volpe

Answer on page 103.

239. Name the last rookie pitcher prior to Will Warren in 2025 who made 30 or more starts in a season for the Yankees.

Answer on page 103.

240. Aaron Judge set the American League record for intentional walks in a single season with 36 in 2025. Name the National Leaguer who holds the Major League Baseball record.

Answer on page 104.

241. Name the Yankees pitcher who won 19 games to lead the American League in 2025.

Answer on page 104.

242. Name the Yankees player who recorded the first 30-homer, 30-stolen base season of his career in 2025.

Answer on page 104.

THE MODERN ERA

ANSWERS

213. B—2009. The new Yankee Stadium officially opened in April 2009.

214. C—Curtis Granderson. Granderson hit 41 homers with 10 triples and 25 steals in 2011.

215. Giancarlo Stanton. Stanton was the first reigning MVP since Álex Rodríguez in 2003 to be traded before the following season.

216. D—John Sterling. Sterling served as the Yankees' full-time radio play-by-play announcer from 1989 to 2023, working over 5,000 consecutive games across a 30-year stretch.

217. A—David Justice. Justice was named MVP after hitting a go-ahead, three-run home run off Seattle's Arthur Rhodes in the decisive Game Six, which the Yankees won 9–7 to take the series, 4–2.

218. C—Gary Sheffield. Sheffield represented the Padres, Marlins, Dodgers, Braves, and Yankees. (Moises Alou has also turned the trick, with the Expos, Marlins, Astros, Cubs, and Giants.)

219. Hideki Matsui. Matsui hit a pivotal three-run home run over the center field wall against Florida's Mark Redman on a 3-0 pitch in the first inning, giving the Yankees a lead on their way to a 6–1 victory.

220. C—Mike Mussina. Mussina retired the first 26 batters he faced and had two outs and two strikes on Carl Everett in the ninth inning before Everett lined a single to left field.

221. Jason Giambi. Giambi hit 209 home runs in his seven seasons with the Yankees from 2002 to 2008.

222. A—Ángel Berroa. Baldelli finished third, Gerut was fourth, and Teixeira fifth.

223. Rafael Soriano. Soriano earned 42 saves in 2012 in place of an injured Rivera.

224. A—Kevin Brown. Brown's record was 211–144 over a 19-year career. He was 14–13 with the Yankees over his final two seasons in 2004 and 2005.

225. D—Chien-Ming Wang. Wang finished second in the Cy Young Award voting in 2006. He won 19 games again in 2007. He suffered a foot injury while running the bases in 2008. The injury was a major factor in the decline of his career.

226. Florida Marlins. Despite winning the award, it was Girardi's only season as the Marlins' manager.

227. B—Mike Mussina. Mussina retired after posting a 20–9 record in 2008.

228. True. Canó had 1,695 hits with the Yankees and Mariners; Nick Markakis was second with 1,651 hits with the Orioles and Braves.

229. A—Fresno State. Following a successful career playing for the Bulldogs, Judge was selected by the Yankees with the 32nd pick in the first round of the 2013 MLB Draft.

230. A—Tyler Austin. Judge immediately followed Austin and went deep against Tampa Bay's Matt Andriese on August 13, 2016.

231. Gary Sánchez. Sánchez extended the franchise record for catchers with 34 homers in 2019. He hit 138 homers during his seven seasons with the Yankees from 2015 to 2021.

232. B—Pete Alonso. Judge hit 52 homers in 2017, passing Mark McGwire's previous record of 49. Two years later, Alonso beat Judge by hitting 53 homers.

233. D—Gleyber Torres. His two All-Star selections before the age of twenty-three put Torres in elite company, as the only other Yankees players to achieve this were Hall of Famers Joe DiMaggio and Mickey Mantle.

234. A—Luke Voit. Voit hit 22 homers in 56 games during the COVID-shortened season.

235. B—DJ LeMahieu. LeMahieu won the NL batting title with Colorado (.348 in 2016) and the AL title with New York (.364 in 2020).

236. Giancarlo Stanton. Stanton hit a game-tying, two-run home run in the fourth inning to help lead the American League to a 3–2 victory over the National League at Dodger Stadium.

237. B—Jasson Domínguez. Domínguez, twenty, homered off Justin Verlander, becoming the youngest player in team history to hit a home run in his major league debut.

238. D—Anthony Volpe. Volpe won the starting shortstop job and a Gold Glove as a rookie in 2023.

239. Doc Medich. Medich started 32 games as a Yankees rookie in 1973; he was 14–9 with a 2.95 ERA.

240. Barry Bonds. Bonds walked intentionally a record 120 times with the San Francisco Giants in 2004.

241. Max Fried. Fried finished in fourth place in the Cy Young Award voting in 2025, behind Tarik Skubal, Garrett Crochet, and Hunter Brown.

242. Jazz Chisholm Jr. Chisholm Jr. hit 31 homers with 31 stolen bases in 2025.

LEADERS OF THE PACK

QUESTIONS

This chapter celebrates the New York Yankees' statistical titans, going beyond the team's numerous championships to illuminate the individual brilliance of the players who redefined what is possible on the diamond and set a standard for greatness that continues to this day. Here we delve into the single-season bests, franchise leaders, and the players who set American League and Major League Baseball records.

243. Which Yankees pitcher holds the franchise record for most strikeouts in a game?

A. Ed Figueroa
B. Ron Guidry
C. Don Gullett
D. Ken Holtzman

Answer on page 113.

244. Which Yankees player set the American League record by driving in 11 runs in one game in 1936?

A. Bill Dickey
B. Joe DiMaggio
C. Lou Gehrig
D. Tony Lazzeri

Answer on page 113.

245. Which pitcher has the most wins in All-Star Game history?
A. Roger Clemens
B. Whitey Ford
C. Lefty Gomez
D. Randy Johnson
Answer on page 113.

246. Which Yankees player holds the Major League Baseball record for hitting the most grand slams in a season?
A. Reggie Jackson
B. Don Mattingly
C. Jorge Posada
D. Bernie Williams
Answer on page 113.

247. Which manager has the most wins in Yankees franchise history?
A. Joe McCarthy
B. Miller Huggins
C. Casey Stengel
D. Joe Torre
Answer on page 113.

248. Which pitcher has the most complete games in Yankees franchise history?
A. Whitey Ford
B. Herb Pennock
C. Red Ruffing
D. Babe Ruth
Answer on page 113.

249. Name the pitcher who has the most wins in Yankees franchise history.
Answer on page 113.

250. During his 12 seasons as Yankees manager from 1949 to 1960, Casey Stengel won 10 American League pennants. Name the National League manager whose record he equaled.
Answer on page 113.

251. Babe Ruth is the Yankees' career leader with 1,852 bases on balls. Which Yankees player is second on the franchise list?

A. Lou Gehrig
B. Derek Jeter
C. Tony Lazzeri
D. Mickey Mantle

Answer on page 114.

252. Which pitcher was the first Yankee to win the Cy Young Award?

A. Bob Turley
B. Ron Guidry
C. Don Larsen
D. Whitey Ford

Answer on page 114.

253. Don Mattingly won the 1984 American League batting title on the final day of the season. Name the teammate who finished second in the race.
Answer on page 114.

254. Which Yankees pitcher is Major League Baseball's all-time postseason wins leader?
A. Red Ruffing
B. Lefty Gomez
C. Whitey Ford
D. Andy Pettitte
Answer on page 114.

255. Álex Rodríguez holds the Major League Baseball record for hitting the most career grand slams, with 25. Whose record did A-Rod break?
A. Lou Gehrig
B. Mickey Mantle
C. Babe Ruth
D. Robin Ventura
Answer on page 114.

256. Which batter struck out 2,597 times in his career, the most in Major League Baseball history?
A. Reggie Jackson
B. Mickey Mantle
C. Babe Ruth
D. Dave Winfield
Answer on page 114.

257. Which player has the most stolen bases in Yankees franchise history?
A. Rickey Henderson
B. Derek Jeter
C. Mickey Mantle
D. Mickey Rivers
Answer on page 114.

258. Name the Yankee who shares the Major League Baseball record with Dale Long and Ken Griffey Jr. of hitting a home run in eight consecutive games.
Answer on page 114.

259. Mariano Rivera is Major League Baseball's all-time saves leader, with 652. Name the relief pitcher who is second on the Yankees all-time list.
Answer on page 114.

260. Name the Yankee who led the American League in batting average during the strike-shortened 1994 season.
Answer on page 114.

261. Which Yankees player set the American League record for most leadoff home runs in a season?
A. Derek Jeter
B. Chuck Knoblauch
C. Kenny Lofton
D. Alfonso Soriano
Answer on page 114.

262. Which pitcher set the Yankees franchise record by appearing in 86 games in 2004?
A. Tom Gordon
B. Mariano Rivera
C. Tanyon Sturtze
D. Paul Quantrill
Answer on page 114.

263. Who is the only pitcher to lead both the American League and National League in shutouts—in the same season?
A. Roger Clemens
B. CC Sabathia
C. Andy Pettitte
D. Randy Johnson
Answer on page 114.

264. Which Yankees player led the American League in runs scored (136) and runs batted in (119) during the 2011 season?
A. Curtis Granderson
B. Jorge Posada
C. Álex Rodríguez
D. Mark Teixeira
Answer on page 115.

265. Two switch-hitters share the record for most games hitting a home run from both sides of the plate, achieving the feat 14 times in their careers. One player was Mark Teixeira. Who was the other switch-hitter?
A. Mickey Mantle
B. Jorge Posada
C. Nick Swisher
D. Bernie Williams
Answer on page 115.

266. Derek Jeter holds the Yankees record for most games played, with 2,747. Which Yankees player is second on the franchise list?

A. Yogi Berra
B. Lou Gehrig
C. Mickey Mantle
D. Roy White

Answer on page 115.

267. Which player was the first player in Major League Baseball history to drive in 100 or more runs in 14 different seasons?

A. Joe DiMaggio
B. Álex Rodríguez
C. Babe Ruth
D. Dave Winfield

Answer on page 115.

268. Which Yankees pitcher was the first pitcher in Major League Baseball history to start a season with a win–loss record of 20–1?

A. Roger Clemens
B. Whitey Ford
C. Randy Johnson
D. Mike Mussina

Answer on page 115.

269. Which Yankees infielder won nine Gold Glove Awards, the most in Yankees franchise history?

A. Clete Boyer
B. Derek Jeter
C. Don Mattingly
D. Bobby Richardson

Answer on page 115.

270. The Major League Baseball record for most win-save combinations is held by the duo of Andy Pettitte and Mariano Rivera, who had 72 such combinations during their time with the Yankees. This broke the previous record of 57 held by Dennis Eckersley and which Oakland Athletics starting pitcher?

A. Tim Hudson
B. Mike Moore
C. Dave Stewart
D. Bob Welch

Answer on page 115.

271. Gerrit Cole led Major League Baseball with 257 strikeouts in 2022, shattering the franchise's single-season record. Whose strikeout record did Cole surpass?

A. David Cone
B. Ron Guidry
C. CC Sabathia
D. Luis Severino

Answer on page 115.

272. Name the team against whom the Yankees hit a franchise-record nine home runs, on March 29, 2025, a game that marked the first time in Major League Baseball history that a team homered on its first three pitches.

A. Baltimore Orioles
B. Houston Astros
C. Milwaukee Brewers
D. Tampa Bay Rays

Answer on page 115.

LEADERS OF THE PACK

ANSWERS

243. B—Ron Guidry. Guidry struck out 18 California Angels during a 4–0 victory on June 17, 1978. The crowd at Yankee Stadium that night began a new tradition of clapping rhythmically each time a batter had two strikes.

244. D—Tony Lazzeri. Lazzeri knocked in 11 runs against the Philadelphia Athletics on May 24, 1936.

245. C—Lefty Gomez. Gomez was the All-Star Game winning pitcher for a record third time in 1937. He also drove in the first run in All-Star Game history in 1933.

246. B—Don Mattingly. Mattingly hit six grand slams in 1987, a record equaled by Cleveland's Travis Hafner in 2006.

247. A—Joe McCarthy. McCarthy won 1,460 games as Yankees skipper from 1931 to 1946. Torre won 1,173, Stengel won 1,149, and Huggins 1,067.

248. C—Red Ruffing. Ruffing pitched 261 complete games with the Yankees from 1930 to 1946.

249. Whitey Ford. Ford won 236 games during his career.

250. John McGraw. McGraw managed the New York Giants for 31 years from 1902 to 1932.

251. D—Mickey Mantle. Mantle was walked 1,733 times during his career from 1951 to 1968.

252. A—Bob Turley. Turley posted a 21–7 record in 1958.

253. Dave Winfield. Mattingly's batting average was .343 to Winfield's .340.

254. D—Andy Pettitte. Pettitte recorded 18 of his 19 postseason wins with the Yankees, and the other with the Houston Astros.

255. A—Lou Gehrig. Gehrig held the record of 23 career grand slams until 2013.

256. A—Reggie Jackson. Jackson also hit 563 home runs with 1,702 RBIs during a Hall of Fame career.

257. B—Derek Jeter. Jeter had 358 stolen bases during his 20-year career. Henderson stole 326 bases in five seasons with the club.

258. Don Mattingly. In 1987, Mattingly homered 10 times over that eight-game span.

259. Dave Righetti. "Rags" saved 224 games during his Yankees career from 1979 to 1990.

260. Paul O'Neill. O'Neill posted a .359 batting average in 1994.

261. D—Alfonso Soriano. Soriano hit 13 homers leading off a game during the 2003 season.

262. D—Paul Quantrill. Quantrill led the American League with 86 appearances in 2004.

263. B—CC Sabathia. In 2008, Sabathia led the AL with two shutouts while with Cleveland, got traded to Milwaukee, and led the NL with three shutouts.

264. A—Curtis Granderson. The Grandy Man hit 41 homers and posted a .916 OPS in 2011.

265. C—Nick Swisher. Teixeira accomplished the feat with three different teams: Texas Rangers, Atlanta Braves, and Yankees. Swisher did it with five teams: Oakland Athletics, Yankees, Chicago White Sox, Atlanta Braves, and Cleveland Indians.

266. C—Mickey Mantle. Mantle played in 2,401 games for the Yankees from 1951 to 1968.

267. B—Álex Rodríguez. A-Rod knocked in 100 or more runs in four different seasons with Seattle, three with Texas, and seven with New York, including 13 years in a row from 1998 to 2010.

268. A—Roger Clemens. Clemens finished the 2001 season with a 20–3 record, winning his sixth Cy Young Award.

269. C—Don Mattingly. Mattingly won five straight Gold Glove Awards from 1985 to 1989 and four in a row from 1991 to 1994.

270. D—Bob Welch. Pettitte and Rivera added nine more in the postseason for a total of 81.

271. B—Ron Guidry. Guidry had 248 strikeouts in 1978.

272. C—Milwaukee Brewers. The Yankees routed the Brewers, 20–9.

FUN FACTS

QUESTIONS

This chapter is a collection of classic lines from Yankees announcers, a potpourri of unusual facts about individual players and the franchise, and some behind-the-scenes stories and clubhouse anecdotes. We'll also test your knowledge of the Yankees' impact on our popular culture.

273. Which former Yankees infielder is referenced in the 1985 music video of Bruce Springsteen's song "Glory Days?"
A. Bucky Dent
B. Graig Nettles
C. Mike Pagliarulo
D. Willie Randolph
Answer on page 125.

274. Which player's uniform number was the first ever to be retired by a Major League Baseball team?
A. Joe DiMaggio
B. Lou Gehrig
C. Mickey Mantle
D. Babe Ruth
Answer on page 125.

275. Which one of the following Yankees has won the most World Series rings?
A. Yogi Berra
B. Derek Jeter
C. Mickey Mantle
D. Babe Ruth
Answer on page 125.

276. Which Yankees player was the only winner of the World Series Most Valuable Player Award to be selected from the losing team?
A. Thurman Munson
B. Bobby Richardson
C. Mariano Rivera
D. Ralph Terry
Answer on page 125.

277. Which one of the following Yankees managers was the only one who never managed in Yankee Stadium?
A. Clyde King
B. Stump Merrill
C. Lou Piniella
D. Bill Virdon
Answer on page 125.

278. Which was the 1978 hit Meat Loaf song for which Phil Rizzuto supplied the baseball play-by-play?
A. "Bat Out of Hell"
B. "Paradise by the Dashboard Light"
C. "Two Out of Three Ain't Bad"
D. "You Took the Words Right out of My Mouth"
Answer on page 125.

279. Name the San Diego Padres free agent outfielder who the Yankees signed to a 10-year, $23 million contract in December 1980, at the time the richest in professional sports history.
Answer on page 126.

280. Which jersey number did Don Mattingly wear before switching to his now-retired number 23?
A. 19
B. 33
C. 46
D. 58
Answer on page 126.

281. Who won a World Series as both a Yankees player and Yankees manager?
A. Joe Girardi
B. Ralph Houk
C. Billy Martin
D. All of the above
Answer on page 126.

282. Who was the only Yankees player to be a teammate of both Mickey Mantle and Don Mattingly?
A. Jim Kaat
B. Thurman Munson
C. Bobby Murcer
D. Roy White
Answer on page 126.

283. Name the player who holds the Yankees record for most stolen bases in a season.
Answer on page 126.

284. Name the first switch-hitter in Major League Baseball history to achieve the batting Triple Crown.
Answer on page 126.

285. Whose uniform jersey number 37 is retired by both the Yankees and Mets?
Answer on page 126.

286. Which Yankees broadcaster helped arrange a meeting between George Steinbrenner and Yogi Berra that brought an end to their 14-year feud?

A. Michael Kay
B. Ryan Ruocco
C. John Sterling
D. Suzyn Waldman

Answer on page 126.

287. Name the last player who was allowed to wear uniform jersey number 42 after Major League Baseball retired it to honor Jackie Robinson in 1997.
Answer on page 126.

288. Which Yankees player was the only Major League Baseball player who ever won a batting title, a Gold Glove Award, and a World Series ring in the same season?

A. Derek Jeter
B. Don Mattingly
C. Paul O'Neill
D. Bernie Williams

Answer on page 126.

289. Name the team for which Joe Torre played when he won the 1971 National League Most Valuable Player Award.
Answer on page 127.

290. Name the Yankees' long-time public address announcer who was honored with a plaque in Monument Park, dedicated on May 7, 2000.
Answer on page 127.

291. Name the first Yankees player who achieved multiple 30-homer, 30-stolen base seasons.
Answer on page 127.

292. Name the Yankees player who hit his 600th career home run exactly three years to the day after he hit his 500th career home run.
Answer on page 127.

293. Which rapper boasted "I made the Yankee hat more famous than a Yankee can"?
A. Drake
B. Eminem
C. Ice Cube
D. Jay-Z
Answer on page 127.

294. Name the first pitcher to start and record the win in each of the clinching games in all three rounds of a single postseason.
Answer on page 127.

295. Provide the nickname given to the group of fans who sit in Section 203 at Yankee Stadium and chant "roll call" at the start of every game?
Answer on page 127.

296. Name the first player to compile over 3,000 hits in his Yankees career.
Answer on page 127.

297. Name the Yankee who was the first player to be unanimously elected to the National Baseball Hall of Fame.
Answer on page 127.

298. Which player was the first Yankees rookie to record at least 20 home runs and 20 stolen bases in a season?
A. Derek Jeter
B. Mickey Mantle
C. Tom Tresh
D. Anthony Volpe
Answer on page 127.

299. Which trade prompted *Seinfeld* character Frank Costanza to berate George Steinbrenner for an ill-advised decision?
A. Jay Buhner for Ken Phelps
B. Doug Drabek for Rick Rhoden
C. Willie McGee for Bob Sykes
D. Fred McGriff for Dale Murray
Answer on page 127.

300. Which of the following is Michael Kay's most recognizable home run call?

A. "Bye, bye, baby!"
B. "It's outta here!"
C. "Kiss it goodbye!"
D. "See ya!"

Answer on page 128.

FUN FACTS

ANSWERS

273. B—Graig Nettles. Springsteen's character, a pitcher, pitches an imaginary game against the Padres, a game he loses because "Nettles got me, bottom of the ninth."

274. B—Lou Gehrig. Gehrig's number 4 was retired on July 4, 1939, the day of his "luckiest man on the face of the Earth" speech.

275. A—Yogi Berra. Berra won an astounding 10 World Series rings in 18 seasons with the Yankees, the most by any player in MLB history. He won three more as a coach and made a total of 21 World Series appearances.

276. B—Bobby Richardson. Richardson starred in the 1960 World Series, won by the Pittsburgh Pirates.

277. D—Bill Virdon. Virdon, the 1974 American League Manager of the Year, helmed the team during their two seasons playing at Shea Stadium.

278. B—"Paradise by the Dashboard Light." Rizzuto claimed not to have realized the innuendo behind his speaking part in a song about teenage lovers in a parked car, but in a 2007 ESPN interview Meat Loaf admitted Rizzuto was in on the joke.

279. Dave Winfield. Winfield hit 205 homers with 818 RBIs during his time with the Yankees. He was elected to the National Baseball Hall of Fame in 2001.

280. C—46. Mattingly wore number 46 in 1982 and 1983.

281. D—All of the above. Girardi won as a player in 1996, 1998, and 1999, and as a manager in 2009. Houk as a player in 1947, 1952, and 1953, and as a manager in 1961 and 1962. Martin won as a player in 1951, 1952, 1953, and 1956 and as a manager in 1977.

282. C—Bobby Murcer. Murcer played with Mantle from 1965–66, and Mattingly from 1982–83.

283. Rickey Henderson. Henderson stole 93 bases in 1988.

284. Mickey Mantle. In 1956, Mantle led the league in batting average (.353), home runs (52), and runs batted in (130).

285. Casey Stengel. Stengel was the Yankees' manager from 1949 to 1960 and the Mets' manager from the team's inaugural season of 1962 until 1965.

286. D—Suzyn Waldman. In 1999, Waldman brought Steinbrenner to the Yogi Berra Museum to apologize to the former manager he fired in 1985, causing Berra to vow never to return to Yankee Stadium.

287. Mariano Rivera. Rivera continued to wear number 42 because players who were already wearing number 42 at the time were permitted to continue wearing it for the rest of their careers, and Rivera was the last active player to do so until he retired in 2013.

288. D—Bernie Williams. Williams achieved the rare trifecta in 1998.

289. St. Louis Cardinals. Torre hit .363 with 137 RBIs that season.

290. Bob Sheppard. Known as "The Voice of Yankee Stadium," Sheppard was at the microphone for over half a century, from 1951 to 2009.

291. Alfonso Soriano. Soriano reached 30-30 in back-to-back seasons in 2002 and 2003.

292. Álex Rodríguez. A-Rod hit number 500 on August 4, 2007, at thirty-two years eight days, and he hit number 600 on August 4, 2010, at thirty-five years eight days, becoming the youngest player to reach both milestones.

293. D—Jay-Z. Jay-Z rapped the line in "Empire State of Mind," released in 2009.

294. Andy Pettitte. Pettitte accomplished the feat during the 2009 postseason against the Twins in the Division Series, the Angels in the League Championship Series, and the Phillies in the World Series.

295. The Bleacher Creatures. The loudest and rowdiest members of the Yankees' fanbase exhibit their devotion to the home team by shouting the players' names in the top of the first inning.

296. Derek Jeter. Jeter notched his 3,000th hit with a home run in 2011. His 3,465 hits place him sixth on the all-time list.

297. Mariano Rivera. Rivera was elected in 2019. Derek Jeter, elected in 2020, fell one vote short of unanimous selection.

298. D—Anthony Volpe. Volpe accomplished the feat in 2023.

299. A—Jay Buhner for Ken Phelps. The fictional Steinbrenner retorts that his "baseball people really liked Phelps."

300. D—"See ya!" Michael Kay has been the play-by-play announcer for the YES Network since 2002. Note: Before that he was John Sterling's partner on radio from 1992 to 2001.